THE GREEK ISLANDS
Genius Loci

Author's acknowledgements

This series of twenty books covering the Aegean Islands is the fruit of many years of solitary dedication to a job difficult to accomplish given the extent of the subject matter and the geography involved. My belief throughout has been that only what is seen with the eyes can trustfully be written about; and to that end I have attempted to walk, ride, drive, climb, sail and swim these Islands in order to inspect everything talked about here. There will be errors in this text inevitably for which, although working in good faith, I alone am responsible. Notwithstanding, I am confident that these are the best, most clearly explanatory and most comprehensive artistic accounts currently available of this vibrant and historically dense corner of the Mediterranean.

Professor Robin Barber, author of the last, general, *Blue Guide to Greece* (based in turn on Stuart Rossiter's masterful text of the 1960s), has been very generous with support and help; and I am also particularly indebted to Charles Arnold for meticulously researched factual data on the Islands and for his support throughout this project. I could not have asked for a more saintly and helpful editor, corrector and indexer than Judy Tither. Efi Stathopoulou, Peter Cocconi, Marc René de Montalembert, Valentina Ivancich, William Forrester and Geoffrey Cox have all given invaluable help; and I owe a large debt of gratitude to John and Jay Rendall for serial hospitality and encouragement. For companionship on many journeys, I would like to thank a number of dear friends: Graziella Seferiades, Ivan Tabares, Matthew Kidd, Martin Leon, my group of Louisianan friends, and my brother Iain— all of whose different reactions to and passions for Greece have been a constant inspiration.

This work is dedicated with admiration and deep affection to Ivan de Jesus Tabares-Valencia who, though a native of the distant Andes mountains, from the start understood the profound spiritual appeal of the Aegean world.

McGILCHRIST'S GREEK ISLANDS

3. SAMOS
WITH IKARIA & FOURNI

Nigel McGilchrist

GENIUS LOCI PUBLICATIONS

London

McGilchrist's Greek Islands 3. Samos with Ikaria & Foúrni
First edition

Published by Genius Loci Publications
54 Eccleston Road, London W13 0RL

Nigel McGilchrist © 2010
Nigel McGilchrist has asserted his moral rights.

ISBN 978-1-907859-02-1

A CIP catalogue record of this book is available from the British Library.

The author and publisher cannot accept responsibility or liability for
information contained herein, this being in some cases difficult to verify
and subject to change.

Layout and copy-editing: Judy Tither

Cover design by Kate Buckle

Maps and plans by Nick Hill Design

Printed and bound in Great Britain by TJ International Ltd, Padstow, Cornwall

The island maps in this series are based on the cartography of
Terrain Maps
Karneadou 4, 106 75 Athens, Greece
T: +30 210 609 5759, Fx: +30 210 609 5859
terrain@terrainmaps.gr
www.terrainmaps.gr

This book is one of twenty which comprise the complete, detailed
manuscript which the author prepared for the *Blue Guide: Greece,
the Aegean Islands* (2010), and on which the *Blue Guide* was
based. Some of this text therefore appears in the *Blue Guide*.

CONTENTS

Samos

Mount Mycale

Strait of Mycale

GREECE
TURKEY
(see Ancient Samos plan)

Based on TERRAIN MAPS cartography
www.terrainmaps.gr

M. Zoodochos Pigi
Kamara
Ag. Zoni
Ag. Paraskevi
Vathy (Samos)
Ano Vathy
Psili
Aminou
Poseidonio

Pythagoreio
Zervou
Chora
Aspidades
Airport
Heraion
Iraio
C. Asprokavos
C. Kolona

Kokkari
Kedros
EC Baptistry
Mytilini
Myli
Pagondas
Batenas
Samiopoula

Kambos
Ag. Mazrona
Vourliotes
Manolates
Kastro
Vourliotes
Lazarou 1025
Koumaradei
M. Megali Panagia

Ag. Konstantinos
Ambelos
Pentalouda
Mount Ambelos 897
Ag. Theodori
Platanos
Kousi
Pyrgos
Neochori
Skoureika
Spatherei

Ag. Dimitrios
Ydroussa
Koimisis
Panagia tou Potamou
Leka
Cave of Pythagoras
Marathokambos
Koumeika
Votsalaka
Kambos
Gulf of Marathokambos

Karlovasi
Potami
Drakei
Mt Kerketeus/Mt Kerkis 1434
Kallithea
Kosmadei
Ag. Kyriaki
Limnionas
C. Ag. Ioannis

Megalo Seitani Bay
C. Katavasi

N

0   5km

SAMOS

Hera—powerful and often difficult Queen of the Heavens—was born on Samos: and that fact meant that from earliest times the island was a particularly important centre of cult, with visitors and suppliants coming to it from all points of the compass. The richness—economic, intellectual and artistic—which this brought to Samos is reflected in the greatness the island achieved in the 6th century BC, and which it has never matched since. At that time, under the firm and ambitious grip of the autocrat Polycrates, the island dominated Aegean waters and established a trade network extending from the Black Sea to Egypt: it had probably the largest marine fleet in the Greek world and boasted a capital city which was unsurpassed by any other Greek city for its size and sophistication at that time, and which was to leave a deep impression on Herodotus when he visited it a century later. The remains of this golden age of Samos are one of the prime reasons for visiting the island. The collection of archaic sculpture from the sanctuary of Hera now in the museum in Vathý, which includes the huge Samos *Kouros*, would be reason enough to come any distance to Samos: for it has no equals outside Athens. Polycrates's ambition

endowed the city with civic and religious structures: a
temple that transformed the very concept of the building
from a glorified hut into a noble structure of impressive
and enduring beauty; a solid harbour mole built out into
the sea through a depth of 60 feet of water; and, most
unusual of all, the tunnel of Eupalinos, which cuts right
through a mountain for just over a kilometre to bring water into the city. In a remarkable combination of technology, geometry and ingenuity, the tunnel was begun from
two sides of the mountain simultaneously and met successfully in the centre: it marks the coming of age in the
Greek world of the application of theoretical models to
the solving of practical problems. In each case, the need
could have been satisfied, or the problem solved, by far
smaller and less ambitious projects; but to say that is to
miss the point, and to fail to understand the joy that the
Early Ancient Greeks took in setting themselves a seemingly impossible project, and then pulling it off. There is
an energy and excitement in this display, akin to the thrill
of seeing a dolphin leaping through hoops. With time,
it calms into the measured maturity of what we call the
'Classical' Age—the far smaller dimensions of the Parthenon, and the sobriety of Polyclitus's sculpture. But no-
where better than on Samos, can the sheer *chutzpah* of
early, 'Archaic' Greece be sensed.

Rich in Antiquity, and still visibly rich today in green-
ness and variety of landscape, Samos, in spite of the
ravages of forest fires in recent years, is still a lush and
beguiling island—both more cosmopolitan and softer
in feel than her more rugged and dowdier neighbours.
Palaeontological finds (displayed in the island's Natural
History Museum) show that Samos always had a rich and
unusual fauna; its flora, today, is still impressive, with
many unique and endemic species to be seen in the island's two mountain massifs, and over 60 different types
of wild orchid recorded. Both this and the island's immense archaeological heritage are not without threat to
their survival: mass tourism is beginning to be a burden
on the island, most of all in the infrastructure and building needed to accommodate it. This is not a recent phenomenon: 30 years ago the airport runway, a large hotel
complex and a rash of other building was permitted to
invade the heart of the areas of archaeological interest
along the ancient Sacred Way—once lined with statuary,
which led nearly 6km from the old port to the Sanctuary
of Hera. Today, the huge ruins of an Early Christian basilica are hemmed in between the putting course and one
of the swimming pools of the hotel complex. Fortunately,
Samos is big enough and grand enough to shrug these
things off, and to delight the visitor with many peaceful

villages of balconied stone houses, and a well-watered landscape which is—but for the repeated fire damage—a walker's paradise.

HISTORY

There has always been an underlying independence and self-sufficiency to Samos, giving rise to a history which has tended to follow a different course from that of the other islands nearby, seeing moments of greatness while others languished, and languishing when others were active. Even in earliest times, it is strange that an island with such richness of natural resources—water, timber, pasture and proximity to the mainland of Asia Minor—has yielded little of significance before the 1st millennium BC. Finds from the Late Neolithic period (4th millennium BC) have been made at Pythagóreio, and there is evidence of a Bronze Age (Mycenaean) presence at, and around, the site of the later *Heraion*: but nothing that presages the extraordinary flourishing of 6th century BC Samos. The island was settled by Ionian colonists, led by Procles from Epidaurus, around 1000 BC. It soon developed its own grain-supplying *peraea* (territory on the mainland opposite), which brought it repeatedly into dispute over boundaries with the cities of Priene and Miletus. The island founded colo-

nies to the north in both the Sea of Marmara and the Black
Sea; to the west, on Amorgos; to the east, on the coast of
Cilicia; and to the south, it participated in the colonies at
Cyrene and Naucratis in North Africa. Already by the 8th
century the island was acquiring dominance in the trade-
routes across the Eastern Mediterranean. Around 638 BC
Colaios of Samos had sailed through the Straits of Gibraltar and beyond, returning safely to Samos with a wealth
that soon became proverbial: his journey was symbolic of
the marine prowess of the islanders. The prestige of the
Sanctuary of Hera increased *pari passu* with Samos's ex-
pansion, attracting lavish dedications from overseas; and
along the commercial trade routes linking Samos with the
Caucasus, Egypt and Mesopotamia, came also an important cultural and intellectual stimulus.

After the overthrow of the tyrant Demoteles in the early 6th century, control of the city remained in the hands
of an élite of landed aristocracy (the *Geomoroi*), until the
emergence of one important family, of more popular
origins: this was the family of Aeaces, and his sons Pan-
tagnotus, Polycrates and Syloson. By killing the first and
exiling the last, Polycrates made himself sole tyrant of the
island around 535 BC. Herodotus has left a vivid account

of Polycrates and his times, and a picture of the greatness to which he took Samos in naval power and architectural magnificence. Polycrates appears to be possessed of the classic combination of charisma, energy and vision, combined with capricious ruthlessness and a bullying— sometimes piratic—visitation of military might on any who got in his way. He courted the king of Egypt, Amasis (XXVIth Dynasty), who at moments appears to have been alarmed by this boisterous new ally; he attracted brilliant people to his court—Anacreon, the lyric poet; Theodorus, the sculptor and metalworker; and Eupalinos, the brilliant engineer of his greatest projects—but he alienated others, most famously the island's greatest thinker, Pythagoras. At the height of his power, he was lured on false pretences to the Asian mainland by the Persian satrap, Oroetes, and was crucified on the slopes of Mt. Mycale, looking across to Samos in 522 BC.

After Polycrates's death, the island languished and lost direction, under the rule of his brother, Syloson, who returned from exile to Samos with Persian support. The Persian influence was resented by the islanders, and Samos participated in the Ionian revolt of 499 BC; it then defected back again to Persia at the Battle of Lade in 494 BC, fought

for Persia at the Battle of Salamis (480 BC), and then reverted once again to the Greek cause at the decisive Battle
of Mycale, in its own waters, in 479 BC For almost 40 years
after, Samos was a member of the Athenian League, pay-
ing its tribute in ships. The disruption caused by a territo-
rial dispute with Miletus led to the island's revolt against
Athenian dominance in 440–439 BC, which was with dif-
ficulty suppressed by Pericles of Athens after a nine month
siege. The terms of the armistice demanded that the walls
of Samos be dismantled, its fleet handed over, and the
city put under direct Athenian sovereignty: in 365 BC the
local population was expelled and replaced by Athenian
clerurchs—colonists with particular and privileged status.
This state of affairs was only reversed when the Samians
returned from exile in 321 BC as a result of Alexander
the Great's decree regarding exiles, put into effect after
his death by his regent, Perdiccas. With the return of its
islanders, Samos saw a new period of growth and stabil-
ity, especially under the Antogonid rulers: probably at the
instigation of Demetrius Poliorcetes, the city's walls were
rebuilt and the gymnasia complex begun. The 3rd century BC saw the island produce two brilliant astronomers,
Conon and Aristarchus; the latter appears to have arrived

at a heliocentric model to explain the movement of the earth in relation to the sun and fixed stars, over 1,700 years before Copernicus formulated a similar hypothesis in modernity. From 281 BC the island was once again an important naval base, this time under Ptolemaic rule: in 129 BC it became part of the Roman province of Asia.

Under Roman rule, the island saw mixed fortunes: in 82 BC a large number of works of art were taken from the Sanctuary of Hera by Verres—so many, that it provoked the indignation of the Roman people. Cicero championed the island's cause in his famous prosecution of Verres, and was later honoured in Samos, together with his brother, Quintus Tullius Cicero, who was Governor of Asia from 61 to 58 BC. Antony and Cleopatra visited the island in 39 BC, perhaps consciously echoing in their relationship that of Zeus and Hera, who had also celebrated their nuptials on the island. Samos seemed to be favoured by the Imperial family of Rome: Augustus wintered on Samos in 20–19 BC, restored some of the sculptures that had been removed and gave the islanders Roman citizenship; Caligula is said to have contemplated rebuilding the palace of Polycrates; Claudius paid for the reconstruction of the Temple of Dionysos; Nero confirmed the island's autonomy.

By comparison with many of the islands further south, the Early Christian community on the island appears not to have been particularly large, and the island may have been all but abandoned in the aftermath of 7th century Arab incursions. In the 10th century, Leo VI 'The Wise', Emperor of Byzantium, created the administrative '*Theme* of Samos', whose seat was at Smyrna; and it was from here that Nikephoros Phokas embarked on his expedition against Crete in 960. The island was allotted to the Latin Emperor after the 4th Crusade of 1204, but within 20 years had reverted to Byzantine government from Nicaea. After 1346 it was under Genoese rule but constant piracy forced the Genoese to move much of the population to their stronghold of Chios over the course of the next century. The Turks captured the severely depopulated island in the 1470s with relative ease. The need for re-colonisation was met in 1572, when the Turkish admiral Kiliç Ali Pasha obtained privileges from Suleyman the Magnificent for those (Christian) settlers who would come to the island from mainland Turkey and Greece. The island's capital was created at Chora. Samos was briefly occupied by the Russians from 1772–24, and played a leading role in the Independence Movement of 1821. Three times the Samian fleet defeated Turkish attempts to land between 1821 and 1824, trouncing a combined Ottoman and Egyptian fleet in August 1824, at the Battle of Gerontas in the Straits of Mycale.

While recognising the independence of Greece, the London Protocol of 1830 excluded Samos from the Greek State; but special privileges and internal autonomy were won by the islanders in 1832, by which Samos paid tribute to the Ottoman Sultanate, but became a self-governing entity, with a Greek prince—the first was Stephanos Vogoridis (1834–50)—and a legislative council of elected islanders, who sat in the new capital at Vathý. Repeated insurrections finally culminated in an acceding to the popular desire for unification with Greece in 1913; the victory was bittersweet because Samos had never before, in all its history, been cut off from its hinterland on the mainland coast opposite; with the exchange of populations in 1923, the rift became permanent. During the Second World War, Samos saw occupation first by the Italians and then by the British; it was heavily bombarded and finally seized by German forces, giving rise to a fierce resistance movement by the islanders.

In the late 1960s the island began adapting its economy to large-scale tourism, a change given impetus by the construction of the airport between Pythagóreio and the *Heraion*. In 2000, devastating fires destroyed almost one third of the area of the island's forests: fires on a smaller scale, since then, have become an almost yearly phenomenon.

The guide to the island has been divided into five sections
- *Samos (Vathý) & the eastern end of the island*
- *Pythagóreio and the Central South of the island*
- *Pythagóreio: Ancient Samos*
    The Sanctuary of Hera
    The port, walls and city
    The Tunnel of Eupalinos
- *The north of the island, Mt. Ambelos and Karlóvasi*
- *The western end of the island and Mt. Kerketéus*

The area between Pythagóreio and the Heraion is so dense in archaeological remains that two sections cover a similar geographical area but in different epochs (recent and ancient, respectively).

SAMOS (VATHY) AND THE EAST OF THE ISLAND

Nomenclature is complicated here. Samos is the official name for the island's capital town, situated on the eastern shore of the deep bay which cuts into the north coast. This is not the site of Ancient Samos, which corresponds to today's Pythagóreio on the south coast. Samos is also the name for the whole island. Since the island has three working ports, this can create confusion when a ferry's destination is given as 'Samos'. To avoid this, the capital and its port are increas-

*ingly referred to as 'Vathý', a name which originally referred
to the older settlement there, on the hill to the south east
of the port. This guide follows the commonest, current us-
age, namely: 'Vathý' for the capital town and its port, 'Ano
Vathý' for its old quarter above the main town, and 'Samos'
only when referring to the island as a whole.*

Vathý sits at the head of a low 'fjord' (Ancient *Panormos*)
surrounded by hills which are green with dense *maquis*.
It is a 19th century working port in origin, and the old
warehouses at its southern end were for storing and ship-
ping the island's two most famous commodities—Samian
wine and tobacco, which was processed here into hand-
made cigarettes, much in demand in Egypt and Turkey.
The **waterfront** is a heterogeneous assemblage of different architectures—the abandoned remains of the 1960s
Xenia Hotel stand next to a handsome, Italianate, **neoclassical mansion** to its right, with heavy rustication on
its corners and an elegant Serlian-arched window looking
onto the water-front; this, in turn, stands next to a simple
house façade with a protruding wooden balcony, redolent
of the ports of Asia Minor and the East. To the north along
the front, is the arcaded and towered front of the **Catholic
church of the Virgin** in French Colonial style, while one
block inland of the waterfront, a different atmosphere

prevails: the narrow alleys, lined with the canopies and wrought-iron balconies of shops and houses, some with courtyards and gardens, has the feel of any busy, Levantine Greek town. It is this mixture of styles, expressing a comparable mixture of cultures, which makes the port at Vathý interesting. The water side of the promenade is dominated by the monument to **Themistocles Sophoulis** (1862–1949), the '*géros*' ('grand old man') of the centre of Greek politics, in the period between the World Wars. He was born on Samos, and was an archaeologist by profession; he entered politics after the First World War and became the leader of the Liberal Party after the death of Eleftherios Venizelos.

The town's principal interest is its exceptional *Archaeological Museum (open daily except Mon, 8–5 summer; 8–3 winter)*, which lies two blocks inland of the centre of the waterfront, at the top of a pleasant municipal garden with palms, fountains and a café. The collection is laid out in two separate buildings, one modern and purpose-built, the other, an adapted neoclassical mansion which was formerly the Paskalion Library. Though cramped and dowdily displayed, this is nonetheless one of the great collections of Greece. It contains antiquities of a wide range of periods; but its **collection of Archaic sculpture** and objects, is its marvel. Archaic art is generally less understood and appreciated than later Classical and Hellenistic art: but few places give a better sense of the energy, optimism and sheer passion of this early period than here—not just the magnificent *kouros*, which is the treasure of the museum, but even the simplest architectural fragments and figurines.

First building

The **first room**, beyond the ticket-desk at the entrance of the modern building, contains a variety of smaller, miscellaneous pieces. Against the right-hand wall are two superb exhibits that reward close attention: an ***ionic capital**, and a ***tri-fold**, '**volute**' (*numbers 6 & 7*)—probably a pilaster-capital from the portico of the temple of Hera. Both pieces are minor elements of constructions, carved anonymously out of an unremarkable local stone in the 6th century BC: the capital furthermore appears to be unfinished behind. But what astonishes is the arresting plasticity and tactile appeal imparted to such workaday elements: in the capital, for example, no deadening straight lines, no flat surfaces, no mechanically drawn circles, mar its design: it has a perfect, natural curvature and plasticity as if it were a soft and living substance inflated with spirit from inside. Alive, not dead; anonymous, not ostentatious; soft, not rigid; sensual, not cerebral. A moment's comparison with the deadness of an unimportant architectural element of a modern building (a door-frame or cornice) shows how a passion for, and absolute understanding of, material informed the 6th century craftsman in even the most insignificant detail of a building.

The **second room** contains some of the best examples—even though fragmentary—of Greece's 6th century BC, sculptural renaissance on Samos. Many still preserve their dedicatory inscriptions (*#16*); some, such as the standing, robed female figure (c. 570 BC) (*#15*) show, by their cylindrical form, how this early sculpture evolved out of the carving of wooden tree-trunks; and all have clear, full volumes underpinning a counterpoint of surface lines and folds: the best example of this perhaps is the beautiful pattern of folds in the formal robes of the ***kore holding a bird*** for offering (*#12*). The room's most important exhibit occupies one whole wall—the so-called *'***Geneleos** group*' (*#22*) after the name of the sculptor who executed the work around 560 BC, and signed his name on the drapery covering the left leg of the left-hand, seated figure. It should be recalled that Hera was the protecting deity of wives, and of marriage, motherhood, and the family: a sculptural group such as this, featuring a husband (reclining right) and wife (seated left), originally framing their three daughters and one infant son, is therefore an appropriate dedication for the Sanctuary of Hera. The group, whose finer details were once coloured in tempera paint, would have lined the Sacred Way that led to the sanctuary. (A copy has been now placed in the archaeological area of the *Heraion*, where it was found.) The reclining father must originally have held an object or animal for offering, or a drinking cup, in his hand, and he rests on a beautifully realised **tasseled cushion**. The figure to his left is a cast of the original statue which is in Berlin: both of the two standing *korai* bear faintly inscribed names— 'Ornithe' and 'Philippe'— as if the group were a covert advertisement for their nubility. With their right hands they slightly lift the drapery of their robes to reveal their feet: their beautiful heads probably found their way, long ago, into a distant, private collection.

Turning the corner into the **third room**, is a revelation. The *****Samos Kouros** is the largest kouros statue to survive from Antiquity—currently 4.7m tall and originally taller, carved in local Samian marble around 575 BC, and still preserving the **dedicatory**

inscription carved down the front of the left thigh: 'Isches, [of the family] of Rhesis, dedicated [me]' Striking above all else is the masterful and simple delineation of forms—the violin-like lines of the space between the arms, and abdomen and hips— an area which is particularly problematic to cut; the brilliant rendering of the **meniscus** of the knee; the volumes of the thorax, shoulders and sternum; and—most extraordinary of all, because it is so hard to predict how it will evolve—the use of the marble's natural **veining** to enhance the modelling of the buttocks and shoulders behind. Once again, the hair and features and details would have been painted: holes still visible in the upper spine were probably for the affixing of a **gold band** which bound the hair above. The face is arresting, and yet serene— the scarcely perceptible smile, reminiscent of faces found in Hindu sculpture. The Ancient Greek word for sculpture is '*agalma*' ('that which gives pleasure and honour'); few pieces in all of Greek sculpture, come closer to fulfilling that meaning than this. The piece was found near the Sacred Way at the *Heraion* in 1980: the floor of the museum had to be specially dug out and made lower in order to accommodate it. Other pieces exhibited in this room (e.g.

the fragmentary thighs of a statue, # 28), show that there were probably other, similar giant *kouroi* statues which populated the site.

ARCHAIC ART IN CONTEXT

Some art aims to describe accurately (later Classical and Hellenistic sculpture does this superbly well); other art re-makes the world according to its own scheme (Cycladic figurines, for example). Archaic art stands on the threshold between these two—stylised and yet convincing, true but still magical. Like so much earlier art, it still works according to a scheme of the appearance of the body; but it has felt and makes us feel, the sensual appeal of the volumes that comprise a body, and of the textiles that cover it. In earlier art, there can be a preponderance of 'pattern'; while in later Greek art, the desire to describe what the mind knows to be there, can sometimes suffocate attention to the sensuality and the sense of order. But in the narrow, chronological window of Archaic art in the 6th century BC, these two tendencies are perfectly balanced. And the balance releases an un-mistakable energy, which can be felt not just in its figurative pieces, but in the abstract ones, too. For this reason it is important to consider the sculpted elements of architecture in this period—friezes, capitals, cornices, etc—to be almost as important as the figure-sculpture itself, for the way in which they express an equally deep response to the sensual appeal of volumes and clear forms.

As with late mediaeval art in Europe, Archaic art is the product of a sophisticated and aristocratic elite; the two share a common emphasis on stylisation, pattern, and elegance. But just as the emphasis on bold volumes and tactile forms in artists such as Donatello and Masaccio in 15th century Florence burst through the limitations of Mediaeval art to create a new, more urgent, visual language, so here, in Archaic art, something similar is happening: the pattern is not just dead pattern, it has vigour and energy; the elegance is not just empty elegance, it is striving for the true proportions and feel of nature. Archaic art has the appeal and inner energy we see again in the earliest Renaissance artists. Just as with them, the moment is only brief; by the middle of the 5th century BC, Greek art has settled comfortably into an easy naturalism from which it never again emerges—

until the arrival of the very different world-view of Early Christian art.

Second building

This part of the museum, converted from a neoclassical library building, exhibits mostly the votive material from the *Heraion*, as well as some much earlier, and some later, objects and sculptures. The ground-floor displays include good explanatory material.

The **Hallway** on the ground floor contains a number of large, headless statues from Hellenistic and Roman periods: quite apart from their style, the extensive use of the running drill to cut much deeper folds in the pleating of drapery dates them to this later period. The **ground floor room to the left** on entering, exhibits the prehistoric and early material. Many of the objects are practical in purpose, such as a wide variety pots for domestic use, and tools made from Milos obsidian; but there are also unusual, **tiny clay altars** of the 3rd millennium BC. A variety of pieces and fragments come from what is always one of the richest sources of material for the archaeologist—the broken refuse invariably found at the bottom of a well. Amongst these are pieces even of marble, Cycladic figurines of the so-called 'violin form'.

The **ground-floor room to the right** gives an overview of the astonishing richness of the Sanctuary of Hera and of the diversity of geographical origin of the votive offerings made to the goddess. The long case against the wall is a chronological display of offerings and casual finds: iron spits for grilling meat, and a bronze cheese-grater(?); a bronze dedicatory inscription, probably attached to a wooden ship; a great many small objects related symbolically to the goddess and her purview—small marble **models of houses** (domesticity); **ivory poppy-heads and pomegranates**, and **bronze pine-cones** (fertil-

ity). There are objects from Cyprus, Egypt (**hippopotami**), Assyria, Babylon, the Caucasus, Iberia, the Italian peninsular, and mainland Greece (a finely-worked **bronze stag**). All these objects date from between the 9th and the 6th centuries BC; in the 5th century, the island lost its former maritime pre-eminence and a perceptible decline set in. There is a brief reprise under the influence of Alexander's liberation of the island in the late 4th century.

The landing of the first floor displays some of the most remarkable finds from the sanctuary, which have survived thanks to the muddy nature of the land at the *Heraion*: these are the *****rare objects in**

wood and ivory. It is not often that such heads and figurines (from Mesopotamia), models of boats, or the lid of a box with its wooden hinge still intact, survive in wood from as long ago as the 7th and 8th centuries BC. In the corner of this area is a particularly fine **funerary stele** depicting a nude youth carrying a box which is masterfully executed in perfect *perspective (note, however, that the stele should be seen from a lower point of vantage than is afforded by its present position). The fluid movement of the fragmentary garlands and drapery of the seated figure partially visible to the left, is typically Ionic in style. This is one of surprisingly few Classical works to be seen on Samos, and dates from the late 5th century BC. Opposite is a case of Byzantine gold coins found by the sea in 1983 on the island's east coast at Megali Lakka, probably hidden by their original owner against a sudden pirate attack.

The two rooms which lead off the landing, exhibit the vast range (and quantity) of votive objects dedicated to Hera from across the then-known world, and show once again how this sanctuary was a thoroughfare—both commercial and stylistic—between east and west. The **room to the right** (south) contains the **bronze artefacts**, many of which were produced in smelting workshops actually at the *Heraion*. The Greeks learned bronze-casting from the Egyptians in the 8th century BC, but soon began to perfect and improve the technology. Show-cases on the far wall display objects of Egyptian origin, amongst them an **engraved mirror**, whose image shows an interesting syncretism of Hera with the Egyptian deity *Mut*. Political and commercial ties with Egypt were particularly important to Samos throughout her history. There is an exceptional quantity of **bronze '*protomes*'**: these are the heads of griffons which were a common element of the decoration of libation-bowls dedicated to the goddess. The bowls, or 'cauldrons', stood on tripods, and the outward facing *protomes*, fixed onto them, possessed the power to avert evil, akin to the mediaeval use of gargoyles. It was perhaps this magical, 'apotropaic' power which saved them from being melted down in later times. Bronze domestic objects (*along the wall of the entrance door*) which were subsequently dedicated to the goddess for whatever reason, were pierced with a stick to render them useless and to signify their sacred dedication—an action akin to the smashing of a toast-glass today. In this section there are **strainers for ritual wine**, and even **bronze bells** which provide an unexpected reminder of the sounds of the sanctuary.

The **room to the left** (north) displays the pottery, ivory and glass objects. The collection of pots (around the walls) is interesting in the way it underscores some of the differences between Ionian ware, and comparable work from mainland Greece. The **Corinthian pottery** is confidently drawn in a high contrast of colours, as opposed to the less-defined **Ionian ware** or the fluid lines and lower contrast of the **Samian ware**. The Cypriot clay figures (*on the short wall by the door*) are recognisable by their characteristic, and strongly modelled, heads. The central cabinets display, **jewellery**, glass, faïence, and some rare and well-conserved pieces in **carved ivory**—finest among them a springing lion, made in Egypt in the 13th century BC, and found at the *Heraion*, to which it had been brought by a visitor over 600 years later. The diversity and provenance of these gifts are impressive: the significance of some of them is mystifying—in particular the 8th century terracotta circle, or *kernos*, for ritual libations, on whose surface stands a heterogeneous assemblage of cups, pomegranates, a panther, a ram's head, and a toad, all realistically modelled in clay.

Next to the museum is the Demarcheion of Samos, with the music school behind, and the church of Aghios Spyridon to the south. This **ensemble of neoclassical buildings**, and the palmy garden in front, were laid out in the years of the city's early prosperity in the last decades of the 19th century.

At the southwest corner of the inlet of Vathý, east of the main junction with the road to Karlóvasi, is the **Museum of Samos Wines** (*open daily, except Sun, from 8–8*), laid out in a formerly active winery beside the water's edge. Lateral rooms display vines, methods of pruning, different presses and torques; the central hall exhibits large wooden, storage and ageing vats—magnificent examples of the **cooper's art**—which stand off the ground above recessed troughs which collect the constant stillicide of condensation drops. Modern artificially cooled *caves*, and a further area below dedicated to the art of barrel-making, can be visited. There is also the possibility of tasting.

SAMIAN WINE

Byron immortalised Samian wine in his carousing refrain from Don Juan: '*Fill high the cup of Samian wine! Leave battles to the Turkish hordes*'. The wine that Byron has in mind was the rich Muscat-grape wine which is produced today; whereas in Antiquity, Samos mostly produced a dry red wine, which found little favour in the Aegean and could not compete with the more highly esteemed production of its neighbours, Chios and Lesbos. Although viticulture on the island goes back at least 3,000 years, there was a moment of discontinuity in the 15th, 16th and 17th centuries when the population of the island dropped dramatically as a result of insecurity and pirate incursions. When the island began to repopulate in the late 1600s a different grape variety—better suited to its soil and climate, as it turned out—was planted: this was the *Moschato Aspro* variety which proved so successful that its sweet, golden, dessert wine became synonymous with the island's name. Red varieties continued to be cultivated until phylloxera decimated the vineyards in 1892, after which predominantly the *moschato* variety was replanted. The small-fruited grape has adapted perfectly to the mountainous areas of the island, with their suitable subsoil, cooler temperatures and long hours of sunshine. The prime area is Mount Ambelos, whose ancient name meaning a 'vine' is confirmation of the antiquity of viticulture here; the best vineyards grow at about 500–600 m above sea level, and in places, even up to an altitude of 900m. The yield per hectare is low, and the grapes are picked over-ripe to give their fullest flavour. The wine has a golden, straw colour, and often a smokey quality to its nose; its pleasure is its complex and lingering, honied, after-taste.

ANO VATHY

A street running inland, perpendicular to the southern part of the waterfront, leads 1 km uphill to **Ano Vathy**, the original settlement of the town, whose narrow winding streets are overhung with wooden balconies projecting from the wood-frame and plaster buildings of a type common to the areas of Ottoman dominion. The most interesting monument is the **double church of Aghii Ioannis Prodromos and Nikolaos**, which is at the top of the village, below the newly created (and copiously indicated) Giannaki Open-Air Theatre. First the church of Aghios Ioannis ('Giannaki') was erected in 1750; then Aghios Nikolaos was added 50 years later. The result is a square and unusually compact profile, dominated by a cluster of four cupolas (two over the combined narthex;

two at the respective crossings). The interiors are currently in bad condition, their 18th century wall-paintings and plasterwork, stained with damp. A rare treasure, though, is the floor of Aghios Ioannis (south), which is laid with patterned **polychrome tiles** in pastel colours, dating from shortly after the church's construction.

AROUND VATHY AND
THE EAST OF THE ISLAND

The eastern end of the island is a landscape of low hills, carpeted in verdant *maquis*, and interspersed with broad valleys which are well-watered and cultivated intensively for olives. The shallow bays and pebble shores are attractive and peaceful. Over all, broods the peak of Mount Mycale (today's Samsun Dağ) on the Turkish mainland across the water to the east, which rises 1,237m directly from the sea. The road north from Vathý, which traverses the residential area of summer villas at **Kalámi**, rounds the cape at the new monastery of the Panaghia Kótsika, and continues with wide views of the Turkish coast to the quiet harbour of **Aghia Paraskeví** (9km). In recent years some rare sightings of the Mediterranean **monk-seal** have been made on this stretch of coast.

The two roads west, which climb steeply above Ano

Vathý, converge on the fertile plateau above, and then split shortly afterwards, with the left-hand branch leading northeast, through the agricultural settlement of Kamára, to the **monastery of the Zoödochos Pigi** ('Fount of Life') (*open daily 10–1, 6–8*) at 7km from Vathý. The last 2km of the road climb through pine-woods with ever widening views, to the monastery buildings which sit low amongst scattered trees on the ridge. The *catholicon* was erected in 1756, using **four monumental ancient columns** brought especially from the ruins at Miletus to support the dome. The deeply wrought and **ornate iconostasis** was made in 1802, and the surrounding monastic buildings were added over the course of the next century to house origi- nally a male community; today, they are home to a small but growing number of nuns. There is a high quality of chant at the sung offices. The courtyard is spacious and well cared for and is entered through an ornate, early 19th-century **gateway** in carved grey and white marble: although the elements of its composition are Orthodox Christian, its florid style is typical of late Ottoman taste and carving.

The belvedere in front of the monastery, with its com- memorative monument, commands an impressive **pano- rama** of the **Straits of Mycale**. It was in these waters—as important as they are narrow, and known in Antiquity as the *Heptastadios Porthmos*—that the Greeks defeated the remains of a Persian fleet in 479 BC, ridding themselves for good of the Persian naval threat. Auspiciously, in the very same waters, the Greek Revolutionary fleet under Andreas Miaoulis defeated the combined Turkish and Egyptian fleets in August 1824. Though quiet today, these narrow waters were much busier in Antiquity. To the south is visible the Bay of Megáli Lákka where the hoard of Byzantine gold coins on show in the Museum in Vathý was found in 1983.

Returning to Kamára, and taking the road south across the valley, brings you to the older **monastery of the Aghia Zoni** (1695) (dedicated to the 'Holy Girdle') immersed in a stand of eucalyptus, plane and cypress trees outside its walls, and jasmine and climbers within. The west front of the *catholicon* is plain, but for a small carved belfry and painted niche; but the interior is entirely covered with 18th-century **wall-paintings**, which are regrettably blackened by soot, and damaged by abrasion and efflorescences. There is once again a richly carved, 18th century iconostasis.

Continuing south from Aghia Zoni, the road rises and falls through a gentle, cultivated landscape of olives and fruit trees, above a pine-fringed shoreline. There are numerous small, white-washed chapels and churches with

schist-slab roofs and plain interiors dating from the 18th
century, a period when there was a resurgence of habitation and cultivation here to supply the growing towns
at the coast. The road ends at **Poseidónio** (12km from
Vathý), an attractive and protected harbour, backed by
olive groves, whose name combined with its critical position on the straits clearly suggests the presence of a temple to Poseidon. Strabo mentions such a temple (*Geog.*
XIV.1.14), saying it is on a promontory opposite the islet
of Narthekis in the channel. This could put the site at any
point from the hill at Psilí Ammos to the promontory
south west of the harbour here. Strabo says that the strait
dividing the island from Asia Minor is seven *stadia* wide.
It is around 1,800m across at this point.

The coastal road west from Poseidónio becomes an
unsurfaced track after 2km, and continues through
a succession of sheltered bays on the north side of the
straits before re-joining an asphalt stretch after 7km,
by the coast, to the west of Psilí Ammos. At this point,
the shore is lagunar in nature, with **reed-beds and salt
marshes**: greater flamingos can generally be seen here in
the winter months, and the surrounding reeds and scrub
are favoured by a variety of breeding warblers, rollers,
and both masked and lesser grey shrikes. In migration
periods there is considerably greater variety of birds to

be seen. The large flats, immediately to the west of Psilí Ammos, were used for salt panning, and took advantage of the seasonal fluctuations of water on the flats for the production of salt. The impressive ruins of the buttressed stone building just behind the shore remain from the **19th-century salt-factory**—its long succession of drying chambers, ventilated by the passage of warm air through the lofts above. **Psilí Ammos** itself is an attractive cove looking onto the straits at their narrowest point: these can best be surveyed from the rise above, beside a monument dedicated to those Samians who have perished in hostilities in different parts of the Asia Minor coast and neighbouring islands.

The road back north from the long sandy beach, west of the salt-marshes, climbs to Drosiá, 500m to the north of which, lies the village of **Palaiókastro**. On a bluff to the left of the road west out of the village, near the chapel of Aghios Tryphonas, are the remains of fortification walls of an ancient settlement. From the main junction beside the three contiguous chapels of Tris Ekklesías just to the west, it is 3.5km back to Vathý centre.

PYTHAGOREIO AND THE CENTRAL SOUTH OF THE ISLAND

Pythagóreio lies on the south coast, 12km from the main port of Vathý; it is the principal port for the smaller ferries, catamarans and hydrofoils that ply the routes south through the Dodecanese. It occupies only a part of the area covered by the Ancient city of *Samos*; in the Middle Ages and up until the 1950s its name was 'Tigáni', a corruption of the Italian word for a warehouse, '*dogana*', which was set up here in the 12th and 13th centuries by Venetian merchants; thereafter it was re-named 'Pythagóreio' in honour of its most distinguished son, the 6th century BC, philosopher, mathematician and spiritual teacher, Pythagoras. The town is almost entirely given over to a seasonal tourism, favoured by proximity to the island's airport and to long stretches of beach. The surrounding area and the port itself contain the most significant archaeological sites on the island, which are the subject of the next sections. This first section will cover points of interest of the post-Antique periods only.

IN AND AROUND PYTHAGOREIO

Overlooking the port and the sea from the only defensible position along this stretch of shore-line—the former acropolis hill to the west—stand the circuit walls of a large 11th-century **Byzantine castle**, which enclose the remains of a Hellenistic villa, and are now partly occupied by the church of the Metamorphosis tou Sotíros. The eastern fortifications and rounded corner towers are excellent examples of the Byzantine constructional technique of stabilising stone walls with densely packed brick-tiles in the interstices. Beside the church is a marble bust to **Lycourgos Logothetis** (né Giorgios Paplomatas) (1772–1850), Samian militiaman and politician who led his fellow islanders in an independence revolt in April 1821. He designed and built the **church of the Metamorpohosis** between 1831 and 1833, to be a memorial of the Battle of Gerontas in the Straits of Mycale in August 1824, and as a thanksgiving for the Greek naval victory there over the Turks.

Though born and educated in Karlóvasi, he passed his later youth abroad and only returned to Samos in his mid-30s having acquired the title 'Logothete' (an archaic Byzantine honorific for a senior administrative official, or 'chancellor') in the court of Romania. He went on to lead the progressive political grouping on the island. He masterminded and participated in the landing on Chios in 1821, in an attempt to force the hand of the neutral Chiots to join the insurrection against Turkey, ultimately provoking the appalling reprisals visited on Chios in 1822. As Samos successfully repelled repeated Turkish attacks (1821, 1824 and 1826) and maintained its autonomy, he established a constitution for the island, and, apart from a spell in prison, was a prominent leader in the productive years until 1834, when Samos was left outside the independent Greek State, and became a semi-autonomous principality under the umbrella of the Sultanate in Istanbul. At this point he went into self-imposed exile, and did not return before his death in 1850.

The tower and castle-buildings to the south and west of the church were all re-built after 1824 to commemorate the Battle of Gerontas, as part of a project of reconstruction, symbolic of the new and special status earned by Samos in the War of Independence.

On the mountain behind the city is another site which was reorganised in the 19th century, but whose antiquity as a place of worship and refuge is considerable. The **monastery of the Panaghia Spilianí** (*1.5km from Pythagóreio, by a right branch from the road leading to the Tunnel of Eupalinos*) occupies a panoramic ledge on the mountainside in front of a broad, shallow cave, whose interior conserves an unearthly cool. In the 1880s the church and buildings in front were re-constructed, and the interior of the cave re-organised: the water tanks and cisterns were placed to collect water from seams to the left, the back wall with its solitary column fragment was closed and plastered, and the small **chapel to the Virgin** was fitted into the wedge-shaped space of the narrow right-hand end of the cave, on the place where the more ancient cult—probably of the Nymphs—preceded it.

Chora and Mytilini

Three-and-a-half kilometres west of Pythagóreio is **Chora**, the unostentatious administrative capital of the island until 1834. Its attractive streets climb steeply to the older area of the village which was built around a powerful spring that gushes from underneath a couple of cafés.

Mytilini, 3km to its north, is similarly an agricultural settlement, spreading to north and south of a *plateia* lined with citrus and plane trees. Its name derives from settlers from *Mytiline*: these could possibly have been the Mytilinians captured by Polycrates and used as the manual labour for his grand building projects, but it is more likely that they were the voluntary immigrants of a later age—in the 17th or 18th century. To the south of the centre is the

Natural History Museum of the Aegean (*open 1 April–31 Oct Tues–Sun 9–2, www.nhma.gr*). Well endowed by the Zimalis Foundation in a modern building, this could be a fascinating museum, given the rich subject-matter, were it not for erratic labelling and an absence of indication of provenance for finds. The **Palaeontological Collection** is the museum's strength, illustrating the range of animals (more than 60 fossilised species) that were to be found in the mountains and pastures of this area, when it was attached to the land mass of Asia, in the Miocene era— antelope, rhinoceros, and a short-necked ancestor of the giraffe, which has only been found on Samos and is consequently known as the '**Samotherium**'. A large number and variety of the skeletons were found in a ravine near to Mytilíní: they date from 6–9 million years ago. The preserved example of a species of tiger, however, which fed off herds of antelope, was captured as late as 1862 in the forests of Samos. It is a timely reminder of how rapidly the fauna of the island has changed over the last century. The museum also contains an interesting mineralogical collection.

From Chora to Pyrgos

Three-and-a-half kilometres west of Chora, a right branch leads up to the **monastery of the Tímios Stavrós**, a late 16th-century foundation, rebuilt on a much larger scale in 1838, when its arcaded outbuildings were added. Yet more impressive for its imposing size is the **monastery of the Megáli Panaghiá**, 2km south along the road to Myli from Koumaradéi (9km from Chora). Once again the *catholicon* is 16th century, while the ornate iconostasis, and the beautifully carved **wooden doors** from the narthex into the *catholicon*, date from the second half of the 18th century. The fortified block of monks' cells (recently restored), with its curious arcades of slightly pointed arches, is also of the same period. Inside the *catholicon*, the surfaces are covered with darkened 16th century paintings. In the centre of the floor a **marble relief** with Adam and Eve plays on the symbolism of the Panaghia ('the Virgin') as the 'New Eve'. Less than a kilometre further downhill, the solitary **church of the Taxiarches** comes into view in the valley below. This is a 14th-century church of compact form, with plain interior: the three conches of it square sanctuary, supporting an octagonal drum, constitute a pleasing complex of volumes and proportions, when seen against the bare slopes of the hillside.

The villages of **Mavratzéi** and **Koumaradéi** lie at the heart of an area, once renowned for its honey production, which was left desolate by the forest fires of 2000, and has only recently begun to recover a new growth of *maquis*.

Because of their proximity to clay deposits, both villages are famous for the production of a local style of pottery. The centre for this diaspora of communities is **Pyrgos** (a further 3.5km west), which sits in the well-watered saddle between Mounts Ambelos (north) and Bourniás (south). The main road through the village is crossed by a raised, **arcaded aqueduct**, constructed in the 18th century during the *Tourkokratia*, to bring irrigation water from springs to the north, across the centre of the village, into the fields south and east of the town. The village is a network of narrow streets, with many traditional stone houses, loosely grouped around a square dominated by the uncompleted shell of the **church of Aghios Giorgios** of 1904: this curious state of affairs may be related to the fact that the village of Mavratzéi, also has a church dedicated to the same saint and constructed in the same year. A temporary chapel, raised within the open central space of the arcaded shell in Pyrgos, has now become a permanent church. The slopes of Mount Ambelos to the north are terraced with fruit trees, olives and vines, and were settled predominantly by Albanians in the two villages of **Mesógeio** and **Pándrosos**. These are tranquil and unaffected villages with many traditional stone-built, balconied houses—some now in ruinous condition. At the western end of the village is the **spring** and communal

wash-house. Beyond Pyrgos to the west, as the views begin to open out over the sea, are the **springs at Koutsi** (*to south side of the road after 3km*) which have given rise to a stand of huge plane trees—survivors of the fires of 2000. There is a pleasant taverna in their shade.

The road due south from Pyrgos, winds through groves of olive and walnut to **Spatheréi** (5km), which extends along a ridge of Mt. Bourniás at 600m above sea level, with expansive **views** towards Foúrni and Ikaría, and a delightful shaded *plateia* at its heart. The road continues round the mountain, now with views south to the offshore islet of **Samiópoula**. The island can be reached by boat either from Pythagóreio or from Marathókambos during the summer months, when it is a popular destination for its clear waters and white-sand **beach of Psalida**; for the remainder of the year the islet is the domain of mountain goats and migrating birds. The upper slopes of this southern face of the island have suffered more, extensive forest-fires; the large **convent of the Evangelistria** (5km south from both Spatheréi and Pagondas), caught in the middle of this, is now in the process of rebuilding.

As the road descends towards Pagóndas from the south, 500m before the village and after a sharp bend, is the **church of Aghios Panteleímon**, set amongst trees in a deep cut in the hillside. This is the site of the **ancient quarry** which provided stone for the buildings of the *Heraion*, which lies 7km east of here at the coast: the church marks just the beginning of an area of quarrying which has radically altered the shape of the north side of the hill opposite. The stone varies from a solid grey limestone, to a grey and white veined marble. St. Pantelemon was the patron saint of labourers engaged in hard or dangerous work, and churches dedicated to him can often be found near to marble quarries; although the church is modern, his presence here is evidence that the quarry was used well into Christian times. The village of **Pagóndas** below, now lives off the cultivation of olives, and there are a number of functioning mills on its perimeter. The large paved and shaded *plateia* is surrounded by cafés that have changed remarkably little in recent times. Many of the prosperous stone-built and **balconied houses** in the area just off the square are abandoned; one—a former school building— is being restored to house a future Folklore Museum.

Visible below, 5km to the east is the village of **Myli** ('mills'), set in well-watered citrus groves on the western side of the Kambos plain: as its name implies, it used water from the Imbrasos torrent to power its mills. The chance finding of a **Mycenaean rock-cut tomb** below the church of Aghios Charalambos (*see below, p. 51*) in the

middle of the village indicates that this fertile and protected area has been inhabited since the Bronze Age: the
Heraion, where a further Early Bronze Age settlement has
been found, is only 2km from here. Equidistant between
Myli and the pleasant, modern coastal resort of **Iraío**, is
a group of buildings to the east of the road, comprising
a fortified mediaeval tower and two churches. The tower
is known as the '*Pyrgos Sarakinis*': 'Sarakinos' means
'Saracen', but this classically occidental stone tower, with
crenellations, a deep machicolation above the entrance,
and rigorously square windows, is unlikely to have been
built by any Saracen. This is a style of building that can be
found in the Cyclades—on Naxos and Andros for example. Even though the structure itself may have been built
a century earlier, the tower is probably named after, and
was used by, Nikolaos Sarakinis, the Patmian sea-captain,
who, together with the Ottoman admiral Kılıç Ali Pasha,
was instrumental in the repopulating of Samos in the late
16th century. The large entrance door which is set here at
ground level is unusual for a building of primarily defensive purpose. Beside the tower is the heavily buttressed,
double church of Aghios Giorgios (north) and **Aghios
Ioannis Theologos** (south). The upper area of the west
front of each church is perforated by a large circular window—an uncommon feature for 16th century church de-

sign. The interiors are simple and plain, but the altar of
Aghios Ioannis Theologos is a superb, **inscribed column**
fragment, surmounted by a **capital**, taken from the area
of the *Heraion*, less than a kilometre from here.

ANCIENT *SAMOS*

THE GEOGRAPHY AND EARLY HISTORY
OF THE AREA

What is called the '*Kambos Choras*' today is a wide
and fertile, south-facing plain between the mountains and the shore. It is watered by the streams that
run off from the mountains to the north (Mt. Ambelos, 1153m) and west (Mt. Bourniás, 778m)—principally the Imbrasos 'river' at the western end, and
the Kaláthi, to the east; today these are only seasonal
streams, but in early Antiquity they probably flowed
more constantly. The mountains protect the plain
from the north winds and create a micro-climate
ideal for cultivation. There were, in ancient times,
two natural harbour-inlets at the far eastern end of
the plain, one where the modern port of Pythagóreio
is, the other—now a small lake called Glyphada—

lies a little to its west (beside the Doryssa Bay Hotel). Between the two was a hill, usable as a low acropolis. There were several strong, fresh-water springs in the area, the most important at Aghiades, to the north of the area, and at Myli, to the west. In short: all the prerequisites for a successful urban settlement.

Given this geography, it is not surprising to find evidence of very early settlement in the Kambos area. On the low hill between the two ancient harbours, where the castle of Lycourgos Logothetis now stands in Pythagóreio, was a Late Neolithic settlement of the 4th millennium BC, whose finds show affinities with contemporaneous Cycladic culture. This hill later became the earliest acropolis and nucleus of the subsequent settlement of historic times. At the site of the *Heraion* itself, where remains of an Early Bronze Age fortified settlement to the north and east of the main temple have been found, and in the village of Myli (2km to its northwest) where a Mycenaean rock-cut tomb can still be seen (in the narrow space between the church of Aghios Charalambos and the school sports-field at Myli), there is clear evidence of a continuous, early habitation and settlement.

But it is the cult of Hera, the queen of divinities, and of her earlier prehistoric forebears in the form of the 'Mother Goddess', that more than anything has determined the development of this auspicious and fertile plain. Since it long predates the evolution of the ancient city of Samos, this guide will begin first at the Sanctuary of Hera, or *Heraion*, and then go on to look at the remains of the city.

THE SANCTUARY OF HERA

The archaeological site of the *Heraion* lies in the southwest corner of the Kambos plain, 6.5km from Pythagóreio (*open daily, except Mon, 8.30–3*). Excavated periodically since the beginning of the 20th century, mostly by the German Archaeological Institute in Athens, this is one of the most thoroughly investigated and documented sanctuaries of the Aegean. Photographs of the site taken during the excavations of the 1950s and 60s show a remarkable density of building foundations and finds, which reveal a relentless superimposition and addition of structures throughout the long history of the sanctuary from Mycenaean, to Roman and Early Christian times. Today, much of this has been covered over again leaving only some of the upper levels of the foundations of structures visible; as a result, the site can appear confusing on a casual visit. One impression never fades, however—the sheer size of the remains of the 6th century BC temple of Hera, which was the last of many temples on the site, and which was begun, and left unfinished, by the tyrant Polycrates. Its predecessor on the site, of comparable dimensions, was already the largest structure of its kind in the Greek world: only the great Temple of Artemis at Ephesus—minimally larger—was to exceed it. It was faced by a magnificent altar and surrounded by a multitude of other sacred buildings which it dwarfed; to a visitor arriving from along the Sacred Way, it would have been glimpsed at the end of a long **avenue of votive monuments** and dedicatory sculptures, which were to be counted, not in their tens, but in their hundreds—amongst them the giant *kouros* now in the museum in Vathý. The sound of peacocks that wandered freely through the sanctuary would have been audible from a distance. Though unknown in Homer's time, peacocks came into the Ancient Greek world shortly after, from India through the medium of the Persian Empire. They were sacred to Hera, and shared with the often brooding and vindictive goddess, a potent combination of consummate beauty and the sound of embittered complaint.

THE CULT OF HERA

It is not known at what point the cult of the Great Mother Goddess, widespread in Asia Minor, was first established on the edge of this plain; but it was probably already 500 years old when Ionian colonists settled here shortly before 1000 BC, and gave to the pre-existing 'Mother Goddess' a more precise identity as 'Hera'. The myth had evolved that she was born amongst the osiers that lined the edge of the Ímbrasos River: Pausanias says that in his time (the 2nd century AD), the '**Sacred Willow**' under which she was born was still to be seen at Samos (*Decrip.* VII.4.4), and he reckoned it to be the oldest tree of any of the Greek sanctuaries (*ibid.*VIII.23.5)—older even than the Sacred Oak of Zeus at Dodona. The tree may have been what is known today as a Chaste Tree, the *Vitex agnus-castus*, a tall, fragrant shrub with lilac flowers which grows in similar habitat, and whose name derives from the fact that it was believed since Ancient times to be a calmant of sexual appetite and a promoter of chastity—though this marries oddly with Hera's favouring of female fertility.

The early Mother Goddess was apparently vener-
ated not in a statue or idol, but in a piece of wood—a
xoanon, or '**wooden image**', described as 'not made
by the hands of man'. This was a not uncommon
state of affairs: the 3rd century BC poet, Callimachus, mentions something similar in reference to the
early cult statue of Athena at Lindos—namely that
her statue was an 'un-worked wooden board' (*Fragment 105*). This in itself is an indication of considerable antiquity and has obvious resonances of earlier
tree-worship. Whether the *xoanon* here was a piece
of drift-wood with an unusually evocative form, or
a board of wood whose natural veining appeared to
delineate an image of the divinity, or whether it was
simply the stump of a sacred tree, we do not know:
there is an understandable reticence among poets
and writers to describe such sacred objects exactly.
In later, historic times, according to Pausanias (*Descrip*. VII.4.4.), there was an image which was the
work of a certain 'Aeginetan, called Smilis ... who
was a contemporary of Daedalus'; it must therefore have been a figure-image at least by that stage.
Whatever its exact form, it was the focus of cult; and

its presence gives rise to the complex history of the architecture in the sanctuary.

THE TEMPLES OF HERA

The remains of Polycrates's unfinished temple are on your left as you enter; its predecessors were situated about 30m to the east of its east front (now covered by the more visible remains of an Early Christian basilica), and the chronological succession of altars stood about 30m further east of that. Archaeological exploration has provided considerable information about the development of the principal sacred building here, which, since it spans the fast evolving period from the 9th to the 6th century BC, encapsulates on one site much of the evolution of the Greek temple-form in general:

- In the **10th century** BC, the site would have consisted principally of a stone altar in front of a Sacred (Willow- or Chaste-) Tree. The focus of cult, the '*sanís a-xoös*', or 'un-sculpted board', in Callimachus's words, was probably beneath or beside the tree; or could even have been the tree stump itself.
- *Temple 1*: With time, this 'image' and others that were

added, needed protection from the elements. There was also need for a place where the more permanent gifts and offerings left in honour of the deity could be stored. As a result of these needs, one of the earliest, large temples in the Greek world was constructed to house the image, in the **8th century** BC, beside the tree—a long hall, 100 Samian feet long (hence its subsequent name, the '*hecatompedon*') by 20 feet wide (c. 33 x 6.6m), with a row of 13 wooden columns down the middle to support the roof. Such a row of central columns inevitably hid the cult image from view, unless it were to be placed—unsatisfactorily—to one side.

- *Temple 2*: Around **650** BC the *hecatompedon* was rebuilt, of the same size, on solid limestone foundations, but this time with a modified interior which resolved the problem of the placing of the image. The columns supporting the roof in the interior were now pushed back to both side-walls and the entrance wall, and formed thereby a running, interior colonnade on three sides, in the form of a Greek Π. The presence also of cylindrical column bases at the corners on the outside suggest that this was one of the earliest examples of a **peripteral temple,** i.e. with an external colonnade and columned entrance porch as well. This colonnade protected the temple's adobe walls from the elements, and provided welcome shade for the crowds who gathered on feast days.

- *Temple 3*: As the wealth and power of Samos increased dramatically, and the international fame of the Sanctuary grew, a much grander temple was planned and begun between **570–560** BC, designed by Rhoecus, and assisted by another artist, Theodorus—the first architects in Greek history, both Samian, for whom we have names. Less than a century had passed, and the conception of a temple had evolved out of all recognition, transforming itself from chrysalis to butterfly. It is not easy to explain the speed and degree of such a development: much has to do with Samos's close commercial and political ties with Egypt, and what the Samians had seen there. There was also the ingenuous desire simply to emulate, or even outdo, the greater and older culture of the Egyptians. For the first time in Greek architecture, the **Temple of Rhoecus** was an edifice in which beauty and grandeur far outpaced function. It was a cage of light and shadow, whose forest of fluted limestone columns, running now in double rows around the *naos*, and rising 18m in height, covered a base that was 105m long, by 52.5m wide—the area defined geometrically by two contiguous, equal squares. It buried the site of the old *hecatompedon*, and extended much further west. It was (as Herodotus claims of its successor) the largest temple of its day. It has itself no precedents, but it was to be the inspiration for a spate of building activity on a massive scale in the Ionian cities, which was then emulated half a century later by the cities of Magna Graecia. These grand buildings (as can be seen from the table below), make the Parthenon in Athens look tiny by comparison. Around 540 BC, the temple of Rhoecus either collapsed, or was shaken by an earthquake, or just became unsafe, and a little over 30 years after it was begun it was dismantled and immediately rebuilt in a modified form and new position.

- *Temple 4*: These are the remains that are seen today. The fact that the new and final Temple of Hera, begun by **Polycrates**, just after **540 BC** and possibly built by the architect and engineer Eupalinos, was moved 40m to the west onto more solid ground, suggests that the earlier temple had manifested problems due principally to subsidence. The move also meant that there was now greater space for ceremony between the altar and the front of the temple. The temple was only slightly larger (108.63 x 55.16m) than its predecessor and was of similar proportions and form; but the inter-columniations were decreased, the columns were slimmed, and their total number increased from 104 to 155. They were almost 20m high, and the **peristyle** which they formed was two columns deep on the long sides, and three-deep at either end, thus breaking and refracting the light and shadow in a manner that was substantially different from the measured effect of a Doric temple, such as the Parthenon. Work on the temple was interrupted at Polycrates's death in 522 BC, taken up again around 500 BC, went into abeyance once more after 478 BC, and resumed in the 3rd century BC, but never with sufficient momentum to complete the building. The columns were never fluted, and neither the floor nor roof completed. Strabo (*Geog.* XIV.1.14), writing in the 1st century AD, refers to the temple as '*hypaethral*', i.e. open to the skies, leaving some doubt as to whether the temple was designed to have an open well of light in its *naos*, similar to the oracular temple at Didyma, or whether he simply meant that no roof had yet been built over it.

On site it is not easy to make immediate sense of the temple remains: what is seen are the raised foundations for the rows of columns that were to bear the weight of the roof. These eventually would have been filled in between with beaten earth and stone and then covered by the marble floor laid above. This means that the steps visible at two points on the east and west of the *naos* may be no more than builders' ramps which would later have been covered over. At many points it can be seen how the dismantled material from Rhoecus's earlier temple—most conspicuously, the **beautifully turned column-bases** with fine horizontal fluting—have been incorporated into the foundations of the new temple as filling. There is a mixture of two materials: a yellowy-white Samian marble (for details and important elements), and a grey local limestone (for walls and steps), predominantly used in the earlier building. The low depression of the central *naos* area, which would have been filled to support the floor, is roughly bisected by the foundations of the western extremity of Rhoecus's temple. The solitary column, unfluted and dislocated by seismic movement, left from the 155 pillars of the original plan, stands only to about *half* its original height: it remains the only visual cue to the extraordinary height of the original building.

The altar

The altar—always the focal point of the sanctuary—has similarly gone through a number of transformations in

COMPARATIVE MEASUREMENTS OF THE LARGER GREEK TEMPLES

Acknowledgements to Henri Stierlin for measurements

Temple & architect	Approx. dates	Dimensions of stylobate	Notes
Samos, 1st Temple of Hera (Rhoecus)	575-560 BC	52.5 x 105m	Collapsed or burned down c. 540 BC
Ephesus, Temple of Artemis (Chersiphron)	560-540 BC	55.1 x 115.14m	Burned down 356 BC, rebuilt later to same size
Didyma, 1st Temple of Apollo	550 BC	42 x 87m	Rebuilt by Seleucus, after 300 BC
Samos, 2nd Temple of Hera, (?Eupalinos)	540-522 BC	55.16 x 108.63m	Unfinished

Temple & architect	Approx. dates	Dimensions of stylobate	Notes
Selinous, Temple 'G' (of ?Apollo or ?Zeus)	510-470 BC	50.7 x 110.12m	
Acragas, Temple of Olympian Zeus	470 BC	56.3 x 113.45m	Unfinished
Athens, Parthenon (Ictinus)	454-432 BC	30.88 x 69.5m	
Didyma, 2nd Temple of Apollo	300-280 BC	51.13 x 109.34 m	Unfinished

its even longer history; but after it was enlarged and redesigned by Rhoecus in 550 BC, it was changed little thereafter. Up until that time, the original altar—reconstructed no less than seven times since the Late Bronze Age—stood at an inexplicably oblique angle to everything else on the same spot: its outline is visible just to the south of the main stack of the 6th century BC altar, which stands today, 60m due east of the temple platform. Today, Rhoecus's altar is a confusing assemblage of decorated flotsam and jetsam: originally it was a monumental structure (38.4 x 18.7m) in the usual form of a wide, Greek *pi*, Π, whose open side directly faced the front of the temple and whose arms surrounded the altar-table proper on its raised platform. Something the structure's *decorative programme, clearly designed and sensuously carved, can be intimated from the fragments of the running friezes with wave-patterns, scrolls, and dart-and-palmette designs. Although these are mostly faithful Roman restorations of the age of Augustus, they are still able to give a sense of the construction's magnificence. A further frieze with exquisite *carved sphinxes (fragments of which are visible beside the modern storehouse to the south)—their wings open and heads facing out, in a manner reminiscent of later seraphim or cherubim designs—crowned the ensemble.

Roman and Early Christian buildings

A standing apse, defiantly abutting the ancient altar, announces a later Christian presence on the site in the form of a 5th century AD **Christian basilica**, constructed almost entirely out of blocks and fragments taken from the pagan buildings—many of them with **inscriptions**. The basilica is fitted snugly in between two pre-existing 2nd century AD, Roman constructions, whose walls and floors it incorporates: a small **Corinthian-style shrine** at its northwest corner and the **Roman temple to Hera** along its south side, built to house the cult statue, while work on the still unfinished great temple languished. There are also the remains of a complex of small, late Roman, **thermal baths** just to the west of the basilica. All these later buildings occupy the sacred space between altar and temple.

To have an idea of how beautifully decorated the Christian basilica was in later centuries, it is necessary to look at the fragments beside the modern storehouse at the south edge of the archaeological area, where a number of carved **Middle Byzantine basket- and wheel-design elements** of rare beauty, belonging formerly to its templon, are propped against the outside wall of the building. Nearby are other entablature fragments from an early Doric structure.

Stoas

Not visible today, but discovered by the archaeologists below the area you have just crossed between the altar and the storehouse, was a particularly early example of a *stoa*—a structure that was later to dominate Greek civic architecture. The roof of the 70m long, **south *stoa* of the** 7th century BC would have been supported by wooden columns, and was positioned (running NW–SE) so as to look onto the bank of the river-course at that time. It was later eliminated by the building of Rhoecus's temple. In the mid 6th century, another, much longer, **north stoa** was constructed along the northern perimeter of the sanctuary, perforated by a gate towards its eastern end.

Votive structures

One thing that impressed Herodotus about this sanctuary was the wealth and variety of its votive dedications. He mentions one piece in particular (*Hist*. IV.152): a bronze vessel, surrounded by '…griffin's heads at the rim, and supported by three kneeling figures in bronze, eleven and a half feet high'. This piece was made from the proceeds of a tithe on the profits of a trading mission undertaken by the Samian mariner, **Colaios**, and was dedicated by him in gratitude to Hera. Colaios's journey was remarkable in that it had penetrated, in the early 7th century BC, into the Atlantic Ocean beyond the Straits of Gibraltar, and had reached as far as *Tartessus*, the area west of Seville—if not substantially further. He returned safely to Samos with a cargo, the profit on which alone was valued at 60 talents. His journey is symbolic of the marine skills, courage and commercial spirit of the 7th and 6th century BC Greeks. A series of stone bases found about 20m east of the south *stoa*, and directly south of the great altar, has generally been interpreted as the support for the **votive dedication of a boat** (a phenomenon encountered elsewhere, e.g on Delos, and on Samothrace). Whether the boat were that of Colaios or not, is impossible to verify.

The only other dedication in this southern area stands on its own, just 10m south of the Early Christian basilica, and is semi-circular in form. It supported the honorific monument erected, around 58 BC to the **Cicero brothers**—in gratitude to the great orator, Marcus Tullius Cicero, who had famously prosecuted Verres (the distinguished art-collector and thief, whose covetous attentions Samos had not escaped) and to his brother Quintus, who was an able and beneficent Governor of Asia from 61 to 58 BC.

Most of the votive monuments, in the form of small temples, treasuries or shrines, however, occupied the northeastern area of the sanctuary. The lay-out of this area is revealing in the way in which the buildings fill the space randomly and are set at different angles to one another, with constantly varying orientations. A sanctuary which develops 'organically' over time cannot necessarily have a master-plan: but the situation here seems to defy even the loosest concept of orderliness.

Sculptures

More clearly visible are the many votive statue bases that
border the Sacred Way, sole remnants of the sculpture
gallery that this avenue once was. Immediately on the
left is the **Geneleos Group** (*see p. 22*), named after the
sculptor who executed the work around 560 BC. These
are casts of the original pieces which have been moved
to the Museum in Vathý. They comprised originally a
complete family group—father (reclining, right) and
mother (seated, left), framing three daughters and an infant son—bearing names inscribed in their drapery, their
clothes and features once brilliantly coloured. The prominent display of his beautiful daughters by a rich aristocrat, at such a conspicuous point of a sanctuary dedicated
to the goddess who promoted and protected marriage, is
probably not without purpose. To the left of the group
are other honorific or dedicatory statue bases; some still
preserve the fixing-dowels or the broken feet of a standing *kouros*, others have their **dedicatory inscriptions**, in-
voking the goddess's name. Directly across the sacred way
from the Geneleos Group is the crescent-shaped base of
one of the sanctuary's most famous dedications, which is
mentioned by Strabo (*Geog.* XIV.1.14). This was a colossal group of three figures—Hercules, being received on
Mt. Olympus by Athena and Zeus—by the 5th century

sculptor **Myron**, known to us best as the creator of the *Discus-Thrower*. Strabo says the sculptures were carried off to Rome by Mark Antony, but later returned again by Augustus, except for the Zeus which he placed in a custom-built shrine on the Capitol in Rome.

The Sacred Way

This kind of **ceremonial avenue**, lined not just with trees but with fine sculptures, is generally found leading into any important sanctuary from the nearest town or point of disembarkation: it was a way of preparing the visitor mentally and spiritually for arrival at the altar and temple. The fine **stone-paved surface**, gently curved for drainage, and bordered by two raised pavements, dates from the Roman era—a period during which the areas to either side were developed with shops and houses, whose foundations can be seen, especially on the south side. Further east, later Byzantine and mediaeval buildings, have encroached right over the side-walks and narrowed the avenue substantially. The marble blocks bearing **inscriptions** continue all the way down; but soon the regular lettering of the Classical inscriptions begins to give way to a later, serifed script of Byzantine inscriptions, carved into the surface of earlier ancient stone pieces. The uncovered stretch of the Sacred Way ends abruptly at the limit of the archaeological site; but its course continues for a further six kilometers following the line of the ancient shore-line, north and east toward the city and port of Ancient *Samos*—today's Pythagóreio. Archaeological investigation is uncovering an **archaic gateway** here, which led in through the eastern boundary-wall of the sanctuary.

THE PORT, WALLS AND CITY

The largest and richest city of the Aegean in the 6th century BC, Samos was still able deeply to impress Herodotus when he visited 100 years later. On his own admission, he digressed at great length about Samian history in his writings, partly because he was so amazed by what he referred to as 'three of the greatest building and engineering marvels in the Greek world' (*Hist*. III. 60), which he was shown during his visit. These were the Temple of Hera, the artificial harbour and its mole, and the kilometre-long tunnel of Eupalinos. The first is discussed above; we now move to the second.

The ancient port

The modern harbour of Pythagóreio (c. 36,000sq. m) is considerably smaller in area than the ancient port (c. 66,000sq. m), owing to subsequent silting and sedimentation on the north and west sides. The original harbour walls on these two sides can be traced today, some way inland of the present water-front. In Antiquity, the wealth of any city in the Greek Islands depended on its ability to manage or dominate sea-trade. Samos had a larger fleet of military and commercial ships than any island city, even Aegina, in the 6th century, and it needed to house them and protect them from the frequent and destructive south winds. Herodotus mentions 'boat-sheds' at Samos (III. 45), and these were probably built by Polycrates in the decade between 535 and 525 BC during the same period in which he upgraded the port. But what caught the historian's attention most was the long **artificial protecting mole**, which ran out to sea across the south side of the harbour, for almost half of a kilometre from its back (west) wall, into a depth of 20 fathoms of water. Laying foundations at such a depth, and building securely on top of them underwater, was an extraordinary feat for those times. It must have been the first example of an endeavour of this kind, on such a scale, and like the first colossal temple of Hera, it was a clear change in thinking from anything that preceded it. The present-day mole dating from 1862, where the ferries dock, is of considerable length; but the Polycratean one was longer and began from further west. It now lies under water, further south out to sea: it is a stone structure made of rubble and re-used architectural material, running for 480m. Only its base exists today, submerged at a depth of 3m near the shore, and at almost 14m at its eastern end, where it begins to turn north and goes beneath the modern mole shortly before its eastern terminus.

In addition, underneath the present north mole of the harbour (which runs north–south), lies a further 6th century BC structure: this was an extension of the land fortifications, and closed the harbour to the east. It is estimated it was about 175m long and 20m wide.

Today's breakwater, enlarged and extended in 1862, would seem to be based on a later (and less ambitious) Hellenistic mole. A 30m stretch of its **neatly cut masonry**, with compact surface and finely-edged borders and paving, is preserved in the space between the taverna, *Várka*, and the houses that front the west of the present harbour. From this point it is possible to follow the projection of its line west for over 150m, past elements of it which are incorporated into recent buildings along the way, until it becomes no more than a cut line in the bedrock towards the end. It terminates in the base of a bastion to the west, where there is a deep hole, as big as a small gateway, cut down through the rock below. Interestingly, Herodotus mentions a secret passageway, leading from the citadel to the sea, in Book III, 147, of his *Histories*. From here the line of the west harbour walls runs inland to the north, parts of which are visible as far as Kanaris Street, beside the Stratos Hotel, in the third block back from the waterfront. Tracing these lines gives a vivid sense of the much greater area of the Archaic harbour by comparison with today's.

The circuit of ancient walls

The energy and manpower that the city threw into upgrading and protecting the port, and the laborious construction of the hidden aqueduct of Eupalinos would have had no sense if there had not also been a closed, protective **enceinte of defensive walls** around the city. At many points—especially on the mountain behind the town—these fortifications are clearly visible and traceable for much of their total length of 6.4km. Only the southern sea-walls are not in evidence. Two distinct campaigns can be distinguished:

1. the earliest walls, erected probably in the 530s BC under Polycrates's rule, were constructed at the lower levels in **polygonal** limestone blocks, and then raised above that level in fired brick and mud; they had few bastions, and mostly arched or **corbelled gateways.** Some of the stone for the western arm

will have been provided by the contemporaneous excavation of the tunnel of Eupalinos; but most of it was obtained from the escarpments to the west of the Panaghia Spilianí, where evidence of **ancient quarries** can still be seen. The defeat of Samos in 439 BC by the Athenians under Pericles led to the forced dismantling of this enceinte under the terms of the armistice.

2. the Hellenistic walls, reconstructed using the foundations of the earlier walls, were built again around 300 BC, under the auspices of Demetrius '*Poliorcetes*' (the 'Besieger of Cities'), this time in **isodomic** masonry composed of large rectangular blocks, often as much as 1.5m long. The enceinte was now endowed with over 30 towers or **bastions** (some square and some polygonal in section), which protected massive **lintel-and-post gateways**, which still preserve the deep slots for fixing the gates. In places these walls were later repaired during the 2nd century BC.

Long sections of the enceinte can be walked—along the east, north and west sides over the hill behind the city. The two periods of walls and gates can be clearly seen and compared in the **eastern sector** above the port (*reached by taking the left turn for Mytiliní, one kilometre out of Py-*

thagórieo, and continuing uphill for 400m until the road returns west to the line of walls). At the **summit** of the hill and down the **western side** (reached from opposite the Doryssa Bay Hotel) the Hellenistic work is relatively well-preserved and displays more clearly the method of its construction: two parallel walls of massive isodomic masonry 3m apart, with stone and rubble in-filling. In the lowest reaches of the western wall, just above the old secondary port of Glyphada, which has now silted up and become an enclosed lake, a **rock-cut ditch** about 3–4m wide runs parallel to the walls 5m to their west (outside); this was left by the quarrying of the stone for the walls, and may have served coincidentally a defensive purpose thereafter. Most impressive of all is the well-preserved **4th century** BC **watch-tower** in the northwest corner which stands to a height of over 10m, with the apertures and precisely drafted corners typical of Hellenistic construction.

Sanctuaries and sites within the walls

The ancient and Early Christian city has been revealed piecemeal by archaeological soundings at many points within and outside the present inhabited area. The areas of interest fall naturally into two groups: a first group follows a line west from the harbour, along the road towards the *Heraion*, roughly following the course of the Sacred

Way; the second group is further inland, scattered on the slopes of the hill of Spilianí to the north, and along the first 100 m of the main road to Vathý. This omits only the remains of the Roman villa and Early Christian churches beside the castle of Lycourgos Logothetis on the south shore of the town, with which we begin here.

The oldest settled area along this sector of the south coast of Samos, of which we have evidence going back to the 4th millennium BC, is the low hill to the west of the port, referred to in Antiquity as *Astypalaia* and today known as 'Kastro'. The hill served as an acropolis for the early city, and may have become traditionally the seat of later rulers' and governors' palaces. Today it is crowned by a restored Byzantine castle (*see p. 41*); the visible ancient ruins here are from the last phases of the site's development in Antiquity. These lie within the circuit of the castle walls, to the east of the modern church of the Metamorphosis; they comprise the foundations of two patrician, **Hellenistic villas** of the 2nd century BC, which appear to have been modified substantially in the course of the 1st century AD and united into one large Roman villa, looking south out to sea and north across the city. The wealth and importance of the building are clear not only from the number of portrait busts and statues of the Imperial families found at this site, but also from the rich

polychrome marbles used for decoration—especially the two exquisite, broken columns of ***Iasos Jasper**, framing an entrance of the north peristyle; other columns in Euboean '*Cipollino*' **marble** can be seen to the east. The villa comprises a series of **colonnaded courts**. Water, as often with Hellenistic and Roman villas, was an important feature: the peristyle court closest to the sea has a complex of water channels within its perimeter, and there is a cistern below an *impluvium* to east of the centre of the area. Samos was a favoured resort by the early Roman Imperial families, many of whom may have stayed here. Antony and Cleopatra are said to have chosen to honeymoon on Samos, perhaps in a conscious and propagandistic emulation of Zeus and Hera whose nuptials were celebrated on the island.

Superimposed on the centre of the area are the rough-stone walls of a small, apsed, 5th century, **Early Christian church**, whose entrance through the north side of its narthex is marked by a monolithic threshold of dark stone (cf. Aghios Ioannis at Melitsácha on Kalymnos); elements of its decorated stonework lie around. At the northern end of the site, sections of the Hellenistic walls are clearly visible; *spolia* from a temple-building of large dimensions are to be seen all around the site.

Along the road from the port to the *Heraion*

Three blocks in from the centre of the harbour front, and one block north of the main street, on Eupalinou Street, is a corner of the *crepis* and fragments of some of the fluted columns of the 4th century BC **Temple of Dionysos**. This has been identified from inscriptions which honour the Emperor Claudius for restructuring the temple after damage wrought by earthquakes in 47 AD. Continuing west along the main street, towards the junction with the road north to Vathý, you approach the area of the ancient *agorá* of the city. To the south of the street, by the junction, are the remains of what is referred to as the **Temple of Aphrodite**, which would have stood in a small courtyard bounded by *stoas* on three or four sides: the stone base of the colonnade (with visible insets for the columns) of the **west *stoa*** can be seen, facing the rear steps of the temple's platform at a distance of 5m; behind it are the lower courses of its back wall. The cult of Aphrodite is attested in this area by votive finds from as far back as the 6th century BC, but the temple whose base is visible today is a Roman construction. There is growing evidence that the Archaic Temple of Aphrodite is being uncovered in excavations just to the north of the main road here; this Roman building, therefore, may be a 1st century temple of Augustus and Roma, which is mentioned in epigraphic sources.

Fifty metres further west along the road and to the
north, behind a first row of buildings, lies what has been
uncovered so far of the ancient ***agorá***, which would have
extended further to the east. The visible remains are mostly of Roman date: a couple of unpolished column fragments in the grey and pink *Africano* marble from Teos, on
the Asia Minor coast opposite Chios, give an intimation
of the colourfulness of some of the buildings which faced
the square of the *agorá*. A little further along the main
road on the same side, and covered by a provisional roof
for protection, is a ***nymphaeum***. On the mountainside
directly above can be seen the Cave of Spilianí, which was
the principle Samian home in Antiquity of the cult of the
Nymphs. The Nymphaeum here was probably a subsidiary shrine combined with a water fountain—a deep pool,
with a hemicycle to the west, faced with sheets of marble,
into which a flight of steps descends. It is probable that
this would have been fed by the water brought into the
city through the tunnel of Eupalinos, which—as recent
archaeological excavations have revealed—was piped and
distributed across the whole inhabited area.

Much of the water from the aqueduct would ultimately have been destined for the area of an extensive 'sports
complex', which occupies a long stretch to the south of
the road west of the nymphaeum, in the low-lying land

between the Sacred Way and the shore. In this area, the few remaining inhabited houses all incorporate spolia and ancient fragments. The **gymnasia**, a *xystos* (covered exercise area) and the **stadium**, appear to have been laid out in the 4th century BC, in the same period that the Hellenistic walls were being built; little remains to be seen on the ground today, except some of the steps of the perimeter colonnade which enclosed the complex, close to the road, and the (western end) **starting-grid**, or *áphesis*, of the stadium which lay in the south of the area and ran parallel to the shore. In between the two peristyle courts for sports practice, the massive block of the well-preserved **thermal baths** (*open daily except Mondays, 8.30–3*) were added substantially later. These are constructed from a wide variety of building materials—large, clean-cut blocks of stone from pre-existing Hellenistic structures, rubble stone walls, mortar, and brick-tiles; originally, this would all have been covered by a revetment in marble or plaster on the interior surfaces. The complex dates from Imperial Roman times, probably the late 2nd century AD; but the building was adapted for Christian use in the later 5th century AD. The northern area has been given over to storing and exhibiting a variety of objects brought here from sites around the town: ancient **altars**, **statue plinths**, **capitals**, **sarcophagus lids** and some fine **stone jars** of a kind similar in design to those adapted for later use as water-stoops in Haghia Sophia in Istanbul. To the south of this, is the area where the Early Christian churches have been constructed over the atrium and *apodyteria* (changing rooms) of the Roman baths: first the plan of a large, apsed structure is seen to the left; then, further in, the foundations of two smaller chapels built over the **octagonal pool** in the centre of the main *frigidarium* of the baths. Masonry still with Roman decorative **mosaic** applied to it is visible to the left. The *calidarium*, or steam-room, lies just beyond its southwest corner, where a marble-lined pool has been consecrated with a cross and turned into the **baptistery** of the Early Christian complex. To the south of here are a succession of three rectangular halls—*tepidaria*—running from west to east, all raised above a sophisticated **hypocaust system**, and with their once marble-clad walls heated through cavities within their thickness, fed with hot air from the furnaces below. The westernmost of these halls, has two **immersion pools** to north and south, and three along its west side. In its southwestern corner is a marble block, immured upside down, bearing an inscription in Greek, to the 'August Tiberius Caesar', suggesting later modification and repair to this part of the building. Further south, overlooking the shore, and running the width

of the building, are the remains of the *palaestra* of the
baths.

Dominating the sky-line immediately to the west are
the imposing remains of a three-aisled, **5th century** AD
Christian basilica, sandwiched improbably between the
swimming pools (west door and narthex) and recreation area (apse) of the Doryssa Bay Hotel, beneath whose
foundations must lie further archaeological remains
(*access is free, either from the shore or through the Hotel's
grounds*). The basilica was almost 30m in length and of
considerable height, as is indicated by the three, soaring,
south piers which still stand today, and which give the basilica its local name, '*Tria Dontia*', or 'three teeth'. There is
no clear evidence that these were mirrored on the north
side, and their position outside of the south aisle suggests
that they were reinforcing buttresses rather than piers
from which sprang a vaulted roof. They are constructed
in rough stone and faced with large blocks of Hellenistic
masonry, dismantled from earlier buildings such as the
Gymnasia to the east. A wide variety of different marbles—Proconnesian, Samian, Iasian—lie around which
will probably have been taken from the adjacent Roman
thermae. The high quality of masonry of the wall perpendicular to the north side of the basilica, constructed in
clear-cut blocks of the 4th century BC, fastened together

with bronze clips, stands out by comparison with the hastily realized, later structures above. A large, contemporaneous, covered drainage channel runs north/south across the west side of the whole site.

Continuing west, past the grounds of the *Doryssa Bay Hotel*, you come to the double-lagoon of **Megáli** and **Mikrí Glypháda**—all that remains of the ancient city's secondary harbour. The presence here of two beached, wooden boats is a reminder of the millennial tradition of boat building on Samos. Supremacy at sea, was not only a matter of building ports to protect valuable fleets, but also of designing more practical and ever-faster ships. One widely-used, military and commercial vessel in Antiquity was called the '*samaina*', and was first developed in Polycrates's Samos. In writing about it, Plutarch emphasises its most important qualities—speed and manoeuvrability:

> the *samaina* is a warship with a turned-up beak,
> like a boar's snout; but it is broader than a trireme
> and has a paunch-like hull, which makes it a swift
> mover, which can also weather a high sea… It was
> first built on Samos … at the orders of Polycrates.
>
> *Life of Pericles*, 26

The boat had sails and two banks of 25 oars on each side, and was generally covered, after the caulking, with a red-lead paint.

To the east side of the inner lake, can be seen the well-preserved isodomic masonry of the **4th century** BC **walls**. To the west is the small **church of the Koimisis tis Theotokou** ('The Dormition'), assembled from, and surrounded by, a variety of Ancient and Early Christian *spolia*, taken from the previous **Palaeochristian church** on the site, which in turn, took pieces from its pagan predecessor. This is the site of the Archaic **Sanctuary of Artemis**, whose temple, which had a roof supported on wooden columns, was early on destroyed by the Persians in 522 BC. Excavation trenches in the marshy area below have yielded a wealth of finds—amongst them the headless *kouros*, with a dedicatory inscription to Apollo, now in the museum in Vathý (*no. 16, mentioned above*). Herodotus recounts (*Hist*. III. 48) how the Samians thwarted the attempt of the Corinthian tyrant Periander to send 300 boys of the nobility of *Corcyra* (Corfu) to Sardis to be made eunuchs, as an act of revenge against the Corcyrans: the party put in at Samos and when the Samians learned the nature of the mission, they were so appalled they confined the boys to the sacred refuge of this Sanctuary of Artemis, saved them from their Corinthian captors, and returned them later to their homes. A **Sanctuary of Demeter** has also been located higher up the hill, just inside the western walls.

To the west of the lakes of Glypháda, were the **cemeteries** of Ancient *Samos*, used continuously from Archaic times (on the hillside further to west) through to Early Christian times (the area immediately west of the Artemision), with the Hellenistic and Roman necropolises between the two. The **Early Christian cemetery** is the most rewarding of these to visit. Its nucleus is an **Hellenistic rock-cut tomb**. Around this, a Christian catacomb seems to have developed early on; as the Christian community grew and began to take over the metropolis, this was then developed into a large urban, cemetery building, perhaps constituting the substructure beneath a chapel above. The way in which it has evolved around an early nucleus suggests a *martyrium*, with the burial place of an important Early Christian figure at its centre. Two levels of **burial loculi** with vaulted roofs or cupolas lead off from the principal arched entrance: traces of colour (principally reds) survive from the decorated plaster of the interiors.

From the port to the ancient theatre

The **Archaeological Museum** of Pythagoreio is currently moving from a small town-house just behind the harbour, to a newly designed building, 200m to the north, at the junction of Eupalinou Street and the main road which climbs out of Pythagóreio towards Vathý; nearly all of the collection is currently in storage. It is not comparable with the museum in Vathý for the wealth of sculpture and votive pieces, but it has nonetheless three areas of strength: **funerary art**, from the finely carved Archaic grave *stelai*, surmounted by Ionic scrolls and palmettes, or *anthemia*, to the later marble sarcophagus, with Ionic pilasters in low relief; the graceful **terracotta figurines** and votive objects from the excavations undertaken at the Sanctuaries of Artemis and of Demeter in the west of the city; and **Roman statuary** from the area of the villa beside the castle of Lycourgos Logothetis—amongst them portrait busts of Augustus and Claudius, and a standing figure of Trajan, with a particularly fine portrait head and traces of under-painting for the purple colour of his deeply folded toga.

The New Museum building itself stands in an area of recent excavation, which has revealed the foundations of a number of **Hellenistic houses**. Almost abutting the museum building in the southwest corner is the peristyle of a large house, marked by standing column stumps: the edges of the central *impluvium* are clearly defined, and the **fine mosaic floor** which surrounds it on all four sides is well preserved. The design with octagonal lozenges on the north side, is particularly beautiful.

Fractionally further up the main road, a turning to the left (north), leads towards the slopes of Spilianí north of the city, on which lie the sites of the ancient theatre and the Tunnel of Eupalinos (1km). The road traverses a wide area which was densely inhabited in Antiquity and now awaits systematic excavation. One example of the wealth of material to be uncovered is the patrician **Hellenistic villa** which has been brought to light, south of the paved road, before the junction leading up to the theatre and to the monastery of Spilianí (600m) (*Currently closed, but can be viewed from outside.*) The house has a long history, stretching from the construction of its water fountain and cisterns (fed by waters from the aqueduct of Eupalinos) in Archaic times, through to repairs and additions made in Roman times; the body of what is seen is Hellenistic— a series of airy rooms facing a central atrium, and areas of **floor mosaics** of exceptional refinement and detail, with a decorative theme of waves and griffons' heads. The **ancient theatre**, 100m to the north of the villa, is covered in a semi-permanent, modern superstructure for musical performances: little remains of its 4th century BC *cavea*, and only the vaulted, Roman, substructure of the stage has survived to any recognisable degree.

The left branch of the road continues 300m further west to the most interesting and significant site of the city, the aqueduct of Eupalinos.

THE TUNNEL OF EUPALINOS (*EUPALINEIO ORYGMA*) AND THE ROMAN AQUEDUCT

The greatest of the 'three marvels' mentioned by Herodotus at Samos (*Hist.* III. 60), and one of the most remarkable engineering feats of Antiquity, is the *Aqueduct Tunnel of Eupalinos (*open daily except Monday 8.45–2.45*), worthy of visit not because it is a 1,036m long, double-tunnel, cut by hand through the mountain—itself a remarkable feat, but nonetheless achievable in the 6th century BC by means of the power of captive, or slave, labour—but because of what it tells us about the rapid evolution of Greek thinking at that time. The fact that the tunnel was begun simultaneously from two points (invisible to one another) on opposite sides of a mountain and met in the centre at a depth of 170m below the surface, with almost negligible margin of error, is an incarnation of the Greeks' extraordinary and evolving ability to solve problems by the application of logic and theoretical imagination to practical situations. Before entering the tunnel, it is worth first recalling the problems and solutions involved in its creation.

Aim and date

Good water is the primary requirement of any city. The quantity (17 cubic metres per hour) and quality of water rising year-round at the spring of Aghiades, 2.5km, as the crow flies, behind the mountain to the north of the city, made it the obvious source for Samos, which was fast growing into one of the largest cities in the Aegean in the 6th century BC. The water from the spring could have been channeled around the slopes of the hill and brought into the city from the west. But the fact that this was not done, and that the much more difficult task of bringing it directly through the mountain was chosen instead, indicates that an external aqueduct was possibly considered too vulnerable to attack by an enemy. It presupposes the existence of the enceinte of walls, to the inside of which the water needed to be safely brought: it also presupposes, as do the walls, an enemy or some imminent threat—most probably the increasing hostility of Persia in the period after 546 BC. This is the logical and accepted reasoning behind the tunnel. But the desire willfully to take on a challenge, or to show bravado in solving a daunting problem, is a fundamental element of the Early Greek character, and should not be excluded as a motivation for an enterprise of this complexity. The size of the giant *Kouros* and of the Temple of Hera, the boldness of the harbour mole, the journey of Colaios into the Atlantic Ocean—all enterprises of the Archaic era—suggest that there were other human impulses at work in the imagination of this extraordinary period, which go beyond a simple consideration of security for a water supply.

Archaeological evidence (potsherds, and the style of masonry in the areas of reinforcement), as well as the testimony of Herodotus, suggest that the tunnel could well have been commissioned by Polycrates, in the same period as the first circuit of walls and the harbour mole(s), i.e after 540 BC—even though some important authorities (notably the archaeologist, Hermann Kienast) put the start of the tunnel around ten years earlier, before the rule of Polycrates. The nature of the threat to Samos was apparently urgent enough to necessitate the bold decision to begin the tunnel from both ends simultaneously, so as to halve the time to completion. It was with that decision that the most interesting problems were raised.

The builders

Herodotus gives the name of the engineer as Eupalinos, son of Naustrophos, from the city of Megara, between Athens and Corinth. 'Eupalinos' is suspiciously similar to the epithet '*eupalamos*', meaning 'ingenious', 'inventive' or 'skillful', and may possibly be a sobriquet given to the architect after the completion of his remarkable works. Megara had a notable tradition of building and engineering: Pausanias admires a famous fountain of Theagenes there (*Descrip.* I. 40.1). It is suggested by Herodotus that the workforce of this endeavour consisted of prisoners of war captured by Polycrates from *Mytiline*, and perhaps settled to the north of the Aghiades spring, in a place which currently takes its name from them—Mytilíní. But it should be recalled that this was not a Pharaonic project in scale: only two men could work on each cutting face at any one time, and the lack of space and of oxygen inside the tunnel, precluded the presence of more than the small number of workers needed to remove rubble and to ferry tools and water to and fro. Estimates vary between 5 and 15 years for the time taken to complete the tunnel; the median of 10 years seems credible, based on the amount of progress possible per day. Eupalinos's design, though perfectly logical, was nonetheless susceptible to human error and unforeseen natural difficulties; the spectre of failure, and its possibly dire personal consequences for him, must have haunted him until the two tunnels successfully met under the mountain.

Problems

The problems inherent in the decision to begin simultaneously from opposite sides of the mountain in the hope
of meeting head-on in the centre, can be summarised as
follows. There is no serviceable landmark visible from
both entrances to the tunnel. The shape of the mountain
does not permit either entrance to be seen from the summit. There were no clocks to verify that a reading of the
angle of the sun's shadow—nature's most reliable measurement—would be taken simultaneously in two different sides of the hill. There were no compasses or theodo-
lites. And it should be remembered that any measure of
direction or level which was made by a series of smaller,
repeated measurements over or around the surface of the
hill, was always subject to a compounding margin of error with every successive measurement taken, especially
over such rough terrain. An error of one degree between
the alignments of the trajectories of the two halves of the
tunnel would result in a divergence of about 9m at the
point where the two tunnels were to meet. Given all this,
Eupalinos had to ensure three certainties in his construction: (1) that the angles of the trajectory were the same
and perfectly aligned so as to guarantee meeting in the
centre; (2) that the two entrances on the opposite sides of
the mountain were perforated at exactly the same height

above sea level; (**3**) that the digging maintained both a constant horizontal level and a straight axial line without deviation. An error in any of these would mean failure. Lastly (**4**), there were purely practical problems, such as the possibility of encountering dangerously unstable rock, or seams of water in the heart of the mountain, which could respectively block or flood the tunnel.

Solutions
The solution to (**1**) was two-fold: first the line of the tunnel had to be mapped over the surface of the hill, and then subsequently projected or extrapolated underground. Mapping and marking a straight line was done by setting up posts covering the 1,500m distance over the hill-top; the straightness of the line is maintained by positioning each new post exactly on the line projected by the alignment of the previous two. Beginning at the top of the hill, from which both the area of the spring and the general position of the city can be seen, it was not difficult to define this straight line: but projecting it underground was more complex. How was this done? If the mouth of the tunnel is taken as one point of reference, then at least one other clearly visible, external point of reference is needed, which can be perfectly aligned with the aperture from inside, as the tunnel progresses deeper, so as to maintain

the correct and constant line of the tunnel. This second external point of reference must also be in absolute alignment with the posts which define the trajectory over the hilltop. This is relatively easy to do on flat land; but, in this case, the terrain drops steeply away at both ends of the tunnel. At the north end, a marker could at least be fixed on the facing slope of the hillside visible across the valley; but at the south (city) end, this was not possible: the land simply dropped towards the sea on this side. So a shaft had to be dug straight down from one of the posts on the surface of the hill to the tunnel below, so as to provide a second point of reference *within* the tunnel. A beam of wood, hung on two ropes down the shaft from a similar beam perfectly aligned with the posts on the surface, provided a further, more exact point of reference for direction: so long as this hanging beam was aligned with a marker in the aperture of the tunnel, the workmen knew, as they looked back from their cutting-face, that their direction of trajectory corresponded to the line of posts on the surface. It appears, in fact, that two such shafts were dug, perhaps for added verification.

If both the groups that were digging were now ready to follow exactly the predetermined alignment on the surface, they would in theory meet—so long as they had begun at exactly the same level—problem (2)—and had continued to dig exactly horizontally. To ensure the same height above sea-level for the point of departure on opposite sides of the mountain, a series of posts was again necessary, this time following the contour of the hill from one side to the other, a distance of about 1,900–2,000m. The posts needed to be in the form of a 'T', with the bar at 90° to the vertical which was set into the ground and verified with a plumb line. The first two or three had to be checked by a water-level; thereafter, each new post had to be exactly at the height of the visual plane defined by the tops of the previous two. The rough nature of the terrain required that this operation had to be repeated hundreds of times. This meant that the compound margin for error was immense. Nothing other than stringent, almost superhuman, meticulousness on the part of the engineer can account for the fact that the difference in level between the two tunnel entrances, over such a distance, is actually no more than 4cm—equivalent to an error of about 1 part in 50,000.

Beginning now to dig into the mountain at the two respective intersections of these two lines of posts—the horizontal and the vertical—guaranteed convergence if an absolute horizontality of cutting and straightness of direction were maintained (**3**). These were the least difficult requirements to fulfill. So long as, respectively, the exter-

nal marker on the hillside across the valley from the north
entry, and the hanging beam(s) down the shaft(s) inside
the south entry, were perfectly aligned with the marker
visible against the daylight of each entrance, then each
trajectory was running straight along the same imaginary
line. To maintain horizontality, standing water or a water
level (the '*chorobates*') could possibly have been used, or,
more likely, a type of hanging sighting-tube which was
used in Mesopotamia, and consisted of a hollow copper
pipe, about 40cm long, suspended horizontally, through
which a sighting can be taken of a fixed marker to ensure
equivalent level. A gentle gradient would eventually be required for the water; but Eupalinos had to construct the
tunnel on a perfect horizontal. To cut it on a gradient ran
the risk of the tunnel flooding and becoming unwork-
able, if a seam of flowing water were accidentally to be
encountered during the digging.

The last, and unpredictable, kind of problem (**4**) which
he faced—areas of unstable rock, which threatened col-
lapse—does appear to have been encountered by Eupalinos, some way in from the north entrance. It was so bad
that it forced him to deviate from a straight line in search
of a more stable area to cut through. This had serious
consequences for him, because it inevitably meant that
the sightline from the cutting-face to the daylight at the

entrance was lost for good, as soon as he deviated. Thereafter, he was literally and metaphorically working in the dark. In correcting his initial deviation, once good rock was again found, he appears to have overcompensated and lost the correct alignment. There was always a risk that the two troops would miss and continue oblivious of one another; now the risk was even greater. To ensure that this did not happen, he devised a simple solution: the trajectory of both campaigns was turned slightly to the same (east) side, so that if the level of each tunnel really were identical, sooner or later they had to cross one another's path; which they did. It is this manoeuvre that accounts for the irregularity of line in the middle of the tunnel. A passage was now open right through the heart of the mountain.

Subsequent completion

Once the two sections of the tunnel were successfully joined, three further works remained. First of all, a channel now had to be excavated with the necessary gradient to allow the water to flow constantly. This was first done to one side of the floor of the tunnel; but it appears that, due to what Kienast sees as a lowering of the level of the spring, a subsidiary tunnel had to be dug below the existing one, at a substantially lower level. This was created by sinking broad shafts down from the side of the floor, approximately every 12m, and connecting them below into a continuous sloping waterway; the southern exit is about 4.7m lower than the northern entrance, representing a gradient of 1:220. This lower tunnel was then lined with terracotta ducts for the water. Next the water had to be brought in a superficial, but hidden, aqueduct from the spring at Aghiades to the north entrance of the tunnel. Finally another aqueduct had to link the southern exit to cisterns and the network of pipes and fountains across the inhabited area of the city. This runs parallel to the hillside and is sunk below ground; the regular shafts used for its construction are visible beside (mostly below, but latterly above) the road which leads to the site.

Armed with this general picture, the following elements may be observed on the visit. The two **vertical shafts** for fixing the direction of the south section of the tunnel can be seen from outside where they sink into the ground— one between the ticket booth and the entrance; the other, just above the entrance building. Of the two, only the second is visible inside the tunnel, at the end of the first stretch of narrow passageway after the steps. Standing in the pool of light it casts, you can see down the length of the tunnel. The sides of the tunnel have a slightly serpentine irregularity, due simply to human error in cutting;

but any deviation is always corrected and the **axial line** remains perfectly straight. The entrance was modified after the original opening became dangerous due to surface erosion; this is why the site is now entered by steps from above, and it means that the daylight from its entrance can no longer be seen from inside. At the foot of the steps you pass through a narrow section between the beautifully constructed, **Archaic strengthening walls**, made in large polygonal blocks, and capped with a pointed ceiling. The body of the tunnel is roughly square in section, on average measuring 180 x 180cm. The limestone walls and ceiling are heavily indented with the striations of the pick. As you proceed down the tunnel, on the right hand side are the regular shafts which drop down to the **lower tunnel** which was connected in both directions from the base of each shaft to form a continuous passage; the waste stone was cleared out through the shaft, and some of it used to fill in the original water-channel which was now not in service. On the floor of the lower tunnel were the **water pipes**— composed of about 5,000 individual segments, interlocking, and sealed together. Hard to detect, but just visible in places, close to the floor on the east wall, are the **engineer's marks**: these are mostly level lines, used to indicate the depth of the trench. Beyond the area that is accessible to visitors, are a couple of inscriptions sketched in red paint; one is a name, '*Asbideo*', another reads '*Parade[i] gma*' ('plan'). The illuminated and accessible sector of the tunnel ends after approximately 250m: rock-fall has now closed the central section. On leaving the site, the **exit of the lower tunnel** which carried the water pipes—at this point, 8m below the upper tunnel—can be seen to the west side below the steps that lead out of the fenced area.

The **north end of the tunnel** presents different aspects of interest. (*This can be reached by foot (50 mins.), directly across the hill-top over which the line of the tunnel was originally traced by Eupalinos; the entrance is low down on the south side of a declivity to your left as you descend into an area of pine-trees. The spring is 15 mins. further to the north/northwest. Alternatively, it may be reached by the road which branches left at the exit of Pythagóreio on the road to Vathý, climbs past the ancient walls, and drops over a brow into the broad valley of the Aghiades spring. The church and spring are found 800m along the road which branches left at the first T-junction. To find the tunnel entrance from the spring: walk back east along the road until there is a rough track bearing to the right, which soon begins to climb steeply up to the right to a crossing of tracks by some pine-trees. The right-hand track from here descends into the dip, on the south side of which is the north entrance of the tunnel, somewhat hidden in undergrowth.*) The **spring of Aghia-**

des, whose abundant waters were the cause of the tunnel-building, rises beneath the **church of Aghios Ioannis**, beside the road in the village of Aghiades. A fragment of a carved, Byzantine *templon* is set in a niche above the church's west door. The church is built directly over the **ancient spring-house** and **cistern**, whose roof—now the church's floor—is supported by a forest of square, marble pillars. The water level in the cistern today is lower than in Antiquity, and the water is ducted directly to Pythagóreio. Immediately to the south side of the church can be seen the beginning of the **closed channel** which bore the water from here to the entrance of Eupalinos's tunnel. A hole in its roof at one point allows the interior to be seen; originally the whole structure was hidden just below ground-level for security. The channel follows the contours of the hill first towards the south, and then making a deep dog-leg east, before sharply returning west again, reaching the tunnel entrance after 900m. Shafts (*whose openings are often hidden and unprotected*) used for the construction of the channel can be located in the course of the last 300m. Walking from the spring to the tunnel affords good views of the remarkable **rock formation** of the hillside to the west, where the long diagonal line of a deep geological fault, has eroded—as if in sympathy—into a natural tunnel running down the entire slope.

The **north entrance** (*currently accessible, though work appears to be beginning on fitting a new gate: torch or flashlight necessary*) has been restored in the last 25 years, but below and to the right is the 'dromos' of the original entrance. Looking back it is possible to see where the external sighting-marker could have been positioned on the shoulder of the rise above Aghiades. The northern sector cuts through a different, and less stable, geological conformation than the southern sector of the tunnel; this has meant that there are two long tracts, 100m in from the entrance, where the walls and ceiling have been reinforced with a facing in cut slabs of stone, similar to that at the south entrance.

A shallow gorge runs southwest (1.5km) from Aghiades to the main Pythagóreio–Chora road, joining it beside a military camp, 2.8km west of Pythagóreio, and a short distance west of the junction for the airport and the *Heraion*. A little after half-way, the gorge is crossed by the ruins of a **Roman aqueduct** of the 1st century AD, built to supplement the tunnel of Eupalinos as the source of the city's water, after the latter had begun to deliver a diminishing supply due to calcification of the pipes and blockage with mud. The source of water which the Romans used was at Myli, 7km west of Ancient *Samos*. The aqueduct runs superficially for a large portion of its overall length, following the contours of the hills: but at this point an arched bridge to cross the gorge was inevitable. The last segment of its water-channel crossed the city from west to east at a level slightly lower than that of the Archaic aqueduct.

ANCIENT TUNNELS

Already common by the 8th century BC in Iran, was a single-ended tunnel, known as a *qanat*, which tapped an underground aquifer and brought water to the surface for irrigation. Such tunnels were constructed by the 'shaft method', i.e. by a series of vertically sunk shafts, the bottoms of which were linked together by short headings underground. Because several work-faces could be opened simultaneously, this was a relatively expeditious method of construction. From Iran, the technology spread to Egypt and was put to service in the oases of its deserts. It came into the Greek world either through the Samians, mentioned by Herodotus (III. 26), who lived and worked in Egypt; or directly from Persia, either brought by Greeks who worked there, or communicated through agents of the king, Cambyses II, with whom Polycrates was in alliance. This 'shaft method', used in the *qanats*, can be seen, applied here on Samos, in the last stretch of tunnel close to the surface, which brings the water from the spring at Aghiades to the north entrance of the main tunnel. Perhaps the most notable example of the technique, however, is the 7km tunnel supplying Athens with water, and built only a couple of decades after the tunnel of Eupalinos; there are other examples at Syracuse and at Lake Copais in Boeotia, where the work was never completed. But the much more complex, double-ended tunnel, employed where the 'shaft method' cannot be applied because the depth of ground is too great, is rarer and slower—because it permits only two simultaneous work-faces. The earliest example is the tunnel on Samos; but, at 1,036m, it is not the longest. An emissary tunnel, 1,600m long, was dug to drain Lake Nemi near Rome at the turn of the 5th century BC; and another, 1,400m long, to drain Lake Albano nearby, begun in 397 BC. In both these Italian examples, the volcanic rock was easier to cut and the depth of the tunnel underground, marginally less: but the achievement is no less astounding for that. The technology was probably brought to the Italian peninsula by the Greeks or through the agency of Carthaginians from Egypt and North Africa, and it was widely applied, first by the Etruscans and later by the Romans. Although no trace of it has been uncovered, the longest ever undertaken in Antiquity would appear to have been that which carried the *Anio Novus* to Rome from the Simbruini hills: it could not have been much less than 2,250m long. A curiosity among Roman double-ended tunnels is that constructed by Nonius Datus at Saldae, in Algeria, which though much shorter and shallower than Eupalinos's, failed to meet in the centre, and required complex machinations to retrieve the situation. The first written, comprehensive source that we possess on the instruments and methods of surveying in Antiquity—although it does not talk about tunnel construction as such—is the 1st century AD work, *On the Dioptra*, by Hero of Alexandria, in which he discusses his design for what is the predecessor of the modern theodolite.

THE NORTH OF THE ISLAND, MOUNT AMBELOS AND KARLOVASI

The north coast of the island is a landscape of pine, plane and cypress, with the two massifs of Mount Ambelos, also called 'Karvounis', (1,153m) and Mount Kerketéus (1,434m) always visible above, and the stony, dark-watered shore below. The coast road alternates in stretches between sea and cliffs, and the mouths of deep ravines, where plane-trees give welcome shade, and in spring nightingales and running water are heard. All along the coastal hillsides, are to be found the traditional, four-square stone houses, with low, hipped roofs and wrought-iron balconies: many are in ruinous condition.

At **Kedros**, 4km west along the coast road from the main road junction (0.00km) southwest of Vathý, are the remains of an **Early Christian cruciform baptismal pool** of the late 4th or 5th century AD (*300m down the right (north) turn after the EKO filling station*), beside the modern church of Aghía Paraskeví. Little else remains of what must have been a basilica and baptistery complex, sited—as so often in this period—close to the sea. The quality of the few fragments of carved marble lying nearby suggests that the surrounding buildings were well endowed with

sophisticated decoration. Beyond Kedros, the coastline
has many attractive, though often windy, beaches, especially those west of Kokkari—Lemonákia and Tsamadoú. **Kokkari** itself (7.5km) is a popular resort, which
has grown up around two rocky coastal outcrops which
overlook a small plain of rich land behind, used for the
cultivation of the onions for which the village is famous.

THE AREA OF KAMBOS, AGHIOS
KONSTANTINOS AND VOURLIOTES

At **Avlákia** (13km), the road, which has been hemmed
between the mountain and the shore, turns west into the
small alluvial plain of **Kambos** (13.5km) at the mouth
of a ravine, and the two **14th century churches** of Aghia
Pelaghia and Aghia Matrona come into view above the
road to the south side, standing out white against the expanse of hills covered in cypress, olive and poplar (*access
by taking the cement track uphill to the south, just beyond
the signed turn for Vourliotes*). Both churches have a central, tri-conch plan, surmounted by an octagonal dome.
For its more compact form, and pleasing contrast of tex-
tures between the whitewashed walls and large-tiled roof,
the lower **church of Aghia Pelaghia** has a more typical
14th or 15th century aspect, but no decorations in the

interior. **Aghia Matrona**, which is 100m further up the track, is extensively decorated with fine 18th century **wall-paintings** in reasonable state of conservation, at least in the upper area and north side of the cupola. Over the aisle, to both sides, are charming depictions of scenes from the Book of Genesis—***Adam naming the animals*** (left) and the ***Expulsion from Eden*** (right)—their emphasis, as often in later Byzantine painting, on narrative line more than on devotional image. The building is larger and more sophisticated in design than Aghia Pelaghia, and has unusual decorative details such as the running dentilation in brick below the eaves.

The shore at Kambos is dominated by the large rectangular structure of an abandoned '*taverna*'—not in its meaning of an eatery, but of a depot for aging and storing wine: this is perhaps the best example of this kind of Samian building, of which there are other examples on the coast at Malagari, 2km west of Vathý.

From the east of Kambos, a subsidiary road, signed for Vouarliótes, climbs south from the shore into the hills; after 1km, a right branch leads to **Pnaka** (a corruption of *pínakas*, a 'picture')—a beautiful, nymphaic spot, where an ice-cold spring of slightly tart, metallic water rises. Returning again to the principal road south, the village of **Vouarliótes** is reached after 5km, immersed in a beautifully treed landscape, high on the north slopes of Mt. Ambelos. As its name implies, the village was created by settlers in the 17th century from Vourla (Ancient *Clazomenae*) in the Gulf of Smyrna on the mainland opposite, who chose the site for its springs, its safe and panoramic position, and its suitability for the cultivation of vines and olives. The village has preserved a strong architectural identity of Asia Minor in its attractive variety of houses, with tiled roofs, long windows, coloured shutters and balconies. Although some of the surrounding area has been damaged by fire, it is an ideal centre for **walking and climbing** the ridges of Mt. Ambelos/Karvounis, and to explore the valleys and villages along the north coast (see *Walking the Greek Islands: Samos etc.* by Dieter Graf, Munich 2005). Only 2 km to the north of the village, the devastation of fires has left the 16th century **monastery of Vrontá** damaged and isolated. Although founded in 1476, and therefore the oldest of the active monasteries on the island, the present buildings—fortified and somewhat inelegant externally, but with graceful arcades surrounding the central *catholicon* inside—date from almost a century later (1566); they were restored in 1960, and will now need more attention, after the recent fires, before the monastic community can return again.

The mountainous area to the south of the monastery

was hidden territory into which the dwindling population of the island was pushed in search of safety from
the repeated seaborne Saracen attacks of the 8th century.
Fortified communities were formed, the late mediaeval
remains of which can still be seen today: 2.5 km beyond
the monastery of Vrontá, on the northeast facing ridge,
at a height of 620m above Kokkari, is the 13th century
structure of the **castle of Loulouda** (*left-hand branch at
junction 800m south of Vrontá; castle is visible on summit to left after 1km*), built on a strategic eminence where
there had been an earlier presence in Antiquity; further
southwest, on a 1,050m peak, half way in distance between Loulouda and the final summit of Mt. Ambelos,
are the earlier remains of **Lazárou Castle** (*5km along the
right-hand branch at junction 800m south of Vrontá*), from
which the **views** across the island to the north, east and
south are yet more dramatic.

Although Vourliótes is perhaps the best known of
them, there are many other villages on these slopes—
Ambelos, **Stavrinídes**, **Manolátes**—which have similarly
interesting architecture, verdurous settings and spacious
views, reminiscent in many ways of the villages of Mt.
Pelion on the Greek mainland. All have springs, streams
and thriving vineyards nearby, and are linked by shaded
roads and paths which converge on the coastal village of

Aghios Konstantinos—where some of the finest plane-trees of the area have found a perfect habitat.

Ydroussa

For 7km west of Aghios Konstantinos, the road follows the shore, until it meets the low expanse of the central valley of the island at Aghios Nikolaos. At this point a branch-road south, leads through the village of Kondakeíka, to **Ydroussa** (4.7km south). Northeast from the main church at the centre of the village, which is decorated inside with 19th century paintings, is a signed track to **Petaloúda**. Turning left at a T-junction after 20 minutes by foot, you continue until the track crosses a stream bed; shortly after this, down a path to the left is the **church of the Koími-sis tis Theotókou** ('Dormition of the Virgin'), standing alone in a shaded space, beside a spring—whose presence suggests there could possibly have been a pagan predecessor on this spot. This is a simple, barrel-vaulted, rural church, of the 12th or 13th century, decorated inside with contemporaneous *wall paintings of exceptional quality, and (except on the ceiling) in good state of conservation, given their age. What impresses most is the quality of the faces, especially in the row of standing saints, and in scenes, such as *Christ raising Lazarus*: they have open faces, with strangely unexpressive eyes, yet with a delicate stylisation of features and hair, and an arresting dignity. The hand of one painter throughout is clear, and his style and the colours he uses, are typical of the very early 13th century. There is a waxy, impasto to his paint preparation, similar to that found in Roman wall-painting, and deriving from an admixture of soap and wax so as to create a mixed **encaustic technique**. This would suggest that the painter may have come from a major artistic centre, if not from Constantinople itself: during the 13th century, the Byzantine rulers still maintained control of Samos from Nicaea. Noteworthy is the **scene of St. Peter** (4th century Bishop) of Alexandria, remonstrating with the tiny figure of Christ in a canopied edicule; the iconography is identical to that in the apse of the church of the Archangel Michael on the acropolis of Tilos. It is an infrequently encountered piece of visual propaganda against the heresy of Arius.

KARLOVASI

The un-Hellenic sounding name is in fact Turkish—*Karlı ovası*, meaning 'place of snowy meadows', perhaps referring to the noticeably white mantle which Mt. Kerketéus wears in certain lights, due to the high chalk content of its bare, upper screes: the city itself, almost as big in population as Vathý, also feels more Levantine than Greek. Only the picturesque quarter of **Palaió Karlóvasi**, overlooking the port from a hill at the western extremity of the city, with its balconied houses, plane trees and tavernas, feels familiarly Aegean. The 'shot-apart' feel of the main city derives from the fact that there is a lot of space here, and the city has spread lazily across the wide mouth of the valley and along the shore: in consequence, it is hard to find its heart. Below the old town is **Ano Karlóvasi**, inland from the sea; on the edge further behind are Meséo Karlóvasi and Neo Karlóvasi; all loosely connected, like the villages of the Attic plain which now have become suburbs of Athens. All these different nuclei have considerable architectural variety, however. The city saw a period of prosperity between 1880 and 1920, based principally on its tanning industry, which took advantage of a local abundance of the acorns and flowing water needed in the process. In 1920 there were 47 tanneries on the island: most of them were here in Karlóvasi, in the area of Riva, east of the port, which accounts for the great number of empty **warehouses** and **tannery buildings** of the 1890s and early 1900s along the water front. They are well-constructed in local stone, with characteristically long windows and tiled, hipped roofs. The mercantile and entrepreneurial families who controlled this industry constructed grand and impressive **neoclassical mansions** inland of the shore, a number of which have survived; the most ostentatious example is now the Samos Headquarters of the *University of the Aegean*, on Panepistímiou Aigaíou Street. The university also possesses another, more restrained, neoclassical building a little further uphill, in a square where there is a ruined, eight-sided **Ottoman fountain**, and the city's small Ethnographic Museum (*currently closed*) opposite. Towards the sea, on Kanari Street, between the large church of Aghios Nikolaos and the shore are later **villas of the 1920s**, and two interesting **bank buildings**, now open to the skies, on opposite sides of the street. With the exchange of populations of 1923 in Asia Minor, and the closing of markets for Greek products in Turkey, the tobacco and tanning industries withered, leaving the city without a viable economy.

West to Potámi

The church known as the **Panaghía tou Potamoú** or, more correctly, of the **Metamorphosis tou Sotiros** ('Transfiguration of the Saviour'), in Potámi Bay, is one of the oldest and most unusual churches on Samos (*1.5km west of Karlóvasi Port*). A track which leads inland from Potámi village up the valley of a stream, passes first the ruins of the early, apsed church of Aghios Nikolaos; after 150m, it reaches the church of the Metamorphosis, whose high bulk of un-rendered stone stands to the left in a beautiful setting among trees. The church has no decoration outside or paintings inside, but is remarkable for its unusual proportions: the floor-plan of the interior is approximately 5m x 5m, while the (inside) height to the 'shoulders' of the building is about 7m , and to the crown of the minuscule cupola, 9m. Four **monolithic columns** in Samian marble, surmounted by finely carved, 5th century capitals support the arches of the crossing; but these do not dictate the height of the building, since they are only a little over one third of its total height. The church was once the *catholicon* of a small monastery complex whose ruined buildings extended to north and south; the vestiges of a baptistery, with an immersion font, can be seen outside the southeast corner, once communicating with the sanctuary through a (now blocked) door in the south wall; the narthex on the front has also gone, exposing the block of the threshold, which is a piece of ancient stylobate that once supported a column. There are Early Christian *spolia* lying nearby, and the columns, capitals, and a fragment of decorated frieze in the church's masonry *templon*, all must come from an important 5th century basilica that stood on or near this site: this may have been destroyed around the 7th century, during the period of Saracen invasions, and the present church built later on its site, in the 13th century. Further into the shaded valley, the path leads to a series of **cascades** and natural pools; another path, climbing steeply up the east slope beyond the church, leads to a small **castle** with a cistern, contemporary with the church below, for which it must have functioned as a vital look-out post.

The roads and tracks all end 2km west of Potamí, beyond which there is 10km stretch of wild coastline where vehicles cannot go, punctuated by the two bays of **Mikró** and **Megálo Seïtáni*—'Lesser' and 'Greater Satan'—although there is an intermittent service to the latter by caïque from the port of Karlóvasi during July and August. It is a 90 minute walk from Potámi to Megálo Seïtáni; but it is rewarded by a bay of exceptional tranquility and beauty, often completely deserted outside of the high season. Chios lies 70 km to the northwest; the shoulder of Mt. Kerketéus rises 1200 m directly behind. The area was designated as a refuge for the endangered Mediterranean **monk seal** over 20 years ago, but discouragingly few have been sighted in this part of the island in recent years.

Inland of Karlóvasi

Although richer in vegetation—citrus, olive and fruit trees—in panoramas, and in undisturbed villages, than in specific monuments the long broad valley which crosses Samos north–south between the two massifs of Kerketéus (west) and of Ambelos (east), is one of the island's most beautiful areas. It is wooded, gentle and cultivated, by contrast with the often barren and dramatic landscapes which lie to the west. Of interest are the two villages of **Leka** (north-west) and **Platanos** (south-east), which exemplify respectively the two types of lowland and upland settlement in the area. Platanos sits on a ridge at 520m above sea-level with unforgettable **views** north to Chios, west to the peaks of the island and south to Foúrni; its *plateia*, with venerable plane trees and a **fountain** of soft water (which incorporates a reused Hellenistic gravestone) set underneath a covered loggia, is one of the most pleasant on the island. One hundred and fifty metres south of the square is the **church of the Koimisis tis Theotokou** (the 'Dormition of the Virgin'). Although much of the building was restored in the 18th century, the original structure is Byzantine, built in the 13th century, as indicated by the marble plaque with the eagle of Byzantium set into the floor, and by carved details of the door between the narthex and the interior. The village, because of its inaccessibility, has always been a favourite hideout of resistance fighters.

THE WEST OF THE ISLAND AND MOUNT KERKETEUS

The west of Samos is dominated by the mass of Mount Ker-ketéus (1,434m), one of the most beautiful and dramatic mountains in the Aegean, which, like Mt. Saos (1,611m) on Samothrace, and Mt. Ochi (1,389m) on Euboea, rises steadily from the sea to the clouds, and shares with them a numinous presence and a pleasing symmetry of form. Its lower slopes are green with broom and olive and fir, and its upper slopes are sometimes so pale from the colour of the chalky, bare rock that the mountain seems covered in a light fall of snow. The surrounding area takes some time to reach from any of the main centres or ports of the island, and has a noticeably slower and more peaceful pace of life. Both the road due south from Karlóvasi, and the main road west from Pythagóreio through Pyrgos, lead into this part of the island. We begin with the latter.

Five kilometres west of Pyrgos, a branch road leads south 1.5 km to the village of **Neochóri** built against the cliff of natural rock in a panoramic position, overlooking a fertile landscape of citrus and olive trees. The tra-

ditional stone buildings and hillside position are similar
to the villages of the north coast, but the light and aspect
are quite different. At the heart of its network of narrow,
precipitous streets is the **church of the Taxiarchis**, with
a fine, carved **iconostasis**, recently re-gilded. In spite of
its name ('New Village'), the settlement here is clearly of
some antiquity, because the deep valley below represented the only pass through the Ambelos massif, across the
centre of the island: there are **sculpted niches**, probably
relating to the cult of the Nymphs, and a rock-cut **6th
century BC inscription** recording the names of the builders of a wooden bridge across the stream at the bottom
of the valley, 1.8 km below Neochori, on the road to **Sk-
ouréïka**. (*The inscription is about 3m off the ground near
the east end of the existing bridge, cut into the rock-face on
the east side of the stream, where it passes through a narrow
gorge.*)

To the west of Neochóri is **Kouméïka**, which has an
Ottoman period, marble **fountain front**, prettily carved
with a mixture of Ancient, Byzantine and Ottoman motifs (palmettes, rosettes, crosses, cypress trees etc). Beyond
extends the wide, south-facing sweep of the **Gulf of Marathókambos**, lined with shingle beaches and shallow waters, backed by olive groves below the protective mass of
the mountain. The succession of villages along its shore

have been developed for a quieter type of tourism than at
Pythagóreio. The village of **Marathókambos** itself sits on
the panoramic lower slopes of the mountain behind, 2km
from the shore, and can also be reached from Karlóvasi
(11.5km), on the scenic road via Leka. From the western
end of the village, 4.2km of unsurfaced track winds west-
wards around the slopes of Mt. Kerketéus to the hermitic
complex of the **Cave of Pythagoras* and the church of
the Panaghia Sarandaskaliótissa. As much for the dramatic beauty of the setting and the deep valley, echoing with
bird song, as for the churches and caves themselves, this is
a visit not to be passed over. Mountains, all over Asia Minor and the Greek world, have always attracted religious
hermits and monastic communities, and Kerketéus, with
its solitude and inaccessible cliffs, is no exception. Many
of the rocks and grottoes in this area are marked by small
whitewashed, stone churches; the most visible is **Aghios
Petros**, crowning a natural rock-stack to the south of the
track, after approximately 2 km.

From the sharp turn in the road in the valley (4.2 km),
the steps lead up towards the sheer rock-face, coming first
to **Aghios Ioannis**, a small 13th century chapel on a ledge
over a small water cistern, once accessible through the
floor of the chapel. From just below the chapel, a rough
track (indicated with red spots of paint) climbs steeply

towards a natural arch, and then round, into the '**Cave of Pythagoras**', which has three chambers leading off a shelf of rock. The legend that Pythagoras took refuge here with some of his students to escape the persecution of Polycrates, before leaving the island for good to settle at Croton in southern Italy, has persisted since earliest times: on hearing it, the 10th century hermit, St. Paul of Latros, came here to live in the cave and to found hermitic communities on the mountain. He probably taught here in much the same manner as Pythagoras himself. Higher up the main foot-path past Aghios Ioannis at the top of a flight of rock-cut steps, is the **church of the Panaghia Sarandaskaliótissa** ('Virgin of the 40 steps'), a single-aisle, stone chapel in the entrance of a deep cave (c. 80m) which dips down steeply into the mountain: about 20m inside, there is a fresh-water pool—one of the primary reasons for hermitic settlement here, in the first place.

PYTHAGORAS OF SAMOS

Universality and exclusivity combine in the life and teachings of Pythagoras in a way which is hard to account for. The famous geometric theorem of Pythagoras is an example of the perfect coherence ('*armonia*') and sacred universality of number and mathematics, and is known the world over; while the exclusive meetings, and the secret teachings, passwords, prescriptions and symbols of the Society he founded, inspired only suspicion and helped to arouse enmity and heap destruction in the end on the Pythagorean sect. The problem arises from the fact that Pythagoras was at the same time both thinker, philosopher and mathematician, as well as a spiritual teacher, seer and leader—although such a distinction between the two would have been hard to make in the 6th century BC, and is a product of our own, post-Aristotelian world-view. Aristotle, who was writing two centuries after Pythagoras, is in fact the earliest source for our sketchy knowledge of the events of his life. Pythagoras left no writings of his own, and a number of those who later recorded things he allegedly said or did, had an interest in ridiculing them. He must have been born around 570 BC, and probably trained on Samos in the craft of his father, Mnesarchus, who was as a gem-engraver: it seems probable that he did travel to Egypt and Babylon since he received, according to Diogenes Laertius, a letter of introduction from Polycrates to

Amasis, Pharaoh of Egypt. It is not hard to see how the worldly and sometimes brutal character of Polycrates might soon come into conflict with an ascetic, religious genius, such as Pythagoras, however: in 530 BC, so as to avoid further conflict with the tyrant, Pythagoras abandoned Samos for Croton in Southern Italy—a destination perhaps encouraged by Democedes of Croton, who was court physician to Polycrates as well as to the Persian emperor, Darius. It is not impossible that he passed some time in the cave here on Kerketéus, while that decision matured. In Croton, led—like his near contemporary Confucius—more by a moral, reforming zeal than by a desire for power, he was drawn into the arena of public affairs, and took a leading role in the politics and expanding influence of the city. Diogenes says he gave it a 'constitution' and, with or through his followers, governed the state so well that it deserved, in a literal sense, the name of 'aristocracy' or 'government of the best'. The influence of such an 'aristocrat' of the soul, and of the societies he formed in neighbouring cities, increased for a good 20 years: but the secrecy and exclusivity of the Pythagoreans' ways, and the assumption of superiority inherent in their behaviour, eventually led to the arousal of popular suspicion and discontent. Pythagoras was either banished or went into exile; meeting-houses were burned, and leading Pythagoreans were rounded up and killed. Pythagoras himself appears to have taken refuge in a Temple of the Muses at Metapontum, where he died, somewhere around the year 500 BC. The immediate influence of his teachings and of the Pythagorean School continued for at least a century more.

Pythagoras seems to have been the first to use the word '*kosmos*'—a word which typifies the genius of the Greek language for combining many potent elements in one concept: a sense of order, right arrangement, coherence, beauty. (Our modern word 'cosmetics' is a distant memory of it.) It is towards unity or empathy with this divine nature of the *kosmos*, that the soul of man aspires. The way was through the purification offered by *philosophia*—a reasoned understanding of the harmony of the *kosmos*—and through sympathy and harmony with all living beings which were of similar substance. Once this central idea is grasped, everything else follows: from the abstention from taking life and of eating animals, and the kinship of all beings through the process of transmigration of souls, to the primacy of pure number as the origin of order and the expression of divine beauty and coherence, and the concept that the perfectly articulated movement of the celestial bodies gave rise to a heavenly music—a music that only the especially enlightened could hear, universal but exclusive. In the process of tracing this grand design, Pythagoras touches upon a variety of observations which are fundamental to later thinking: not just the way in which pure number and order are incarnate in the physical relationships of spatial geometry, as expressed in the Theorem that bears his name, but their immediate presence to the senses in the harmony of musical intervals. Nothing is perhaps more central to his philosophy than the revelation that the indisputable perfection of harmonic intervals (the musical octave, the fifth and the fourth) was yet another expression of pure number ratios (2:1, 3:2, and 4:3), provable by the measurement of lengths of musical strings. For Pythagoras, this did not remain a question of detached analysis: it was tangible proof that our world was alive and imbued with a divine and mysterious beauty and order—that it was a *kosmos* in the truest sense of the word.

From below the cave, the track continues back down the gorge to the south coast (3.5 km), meeting the road along the shore which continues west, passing the attractive sandy beach of Psilí Ammos, towards **Limniónas** (9km), a beautifully sheltered bay offering good accommodation (see *Lodging* below) which complements the beauty and tranquillity of the setting. Beyond the village of Aghia Kyriakí (9 km), the road climbs steeply through rocky scrub and olive, to a rise (13 km) where sudden and spectacular **views** of Foúrni and Ikaría open across the water below. From this point on, there is little traffic or concentrated habitation, and even the principal villages, **Kallithéa** (19km) and **Drakéi** (25km) have an air of lassitude and remote abandon—compensated for by their enviable positions and views. There are many fine coves: both to the north at **Varsamo** and **Aghios Isidoros**; and to the south, at the bays of Klima and Aghiánni (4km south of the main road, via Palaiochori), where the mid-19th century **monastery of Aghios Ioannis Eleïmonos** ('St. John the Giver of Help'), sits in a shaded and well-watered hollow above the shore, looking onto the small islet of Katergo.

The most significant monuments in this area are the **cave churches** on the western slope of Kerketéus, above Kallithéa. (*An unsurfaced road leads up from the cemetery at the southern end of Kallithéa; after 1.7km, a left turn at the junction climbs steeply a further 2km to the church of Aghia Paraskeví, from where a footpath leads uphill 1 km east, to the first of the churches.*) The **church of the Panaghia Makriní** sits sunk a little into the entrance of a shallow cave. The original 13th century chapel was incorporated and expanded in the 18th century, into the larger tri-conch structure with cupola which you enter first, but still preserves its original **wall-paintings**: their condition is deteriorating, but some of the original, intense colour is still visible in the gracious figure of the Virgin Mary, in the south east corner. At **Aghia Triada**, a short distance further up the path, the church, behind a simple front, is created out of the natural rock of the cave. Below the village of Kallithéa to the southeast, is the **church of Aghios Charalambos** with an interior extensively decorated with 18th century wall-paintings.

'*Kerkis*', the modern Greek name of the mountain, is the ancient Greek word (meaning a 'weaver's shuttle') used for the 'Judas Tree' or 'Eastern Redbud', which still

populates the mountain's northern slopes. **Mount Kerketéus**, however, is rich in many endemic, or even unique,
species of plant. At the highest altitudes (above 1,200m)
among the limestone crevices, the perennial spiny knap-
weed, *Centaurea xylobasis*, can be found only here; while
lower down on the gravel screes, the rare, delicate, lilac-
flowered larkspur, *Consolida samia*, and, on the floors of
the pinewoods, *Muscari kerkis*, a violet-coloured grape-
hyacinth, are unique to the island and the mountain, as
their names imply. Samos is also rich in orchids, with over
60 species recorded—*Ophrys icariensis* and *O. minutula*,
being endemic to the islands of this area. Mount Ambelos
has its own particular flora also: a number of unusual cro-
cuses (the orange *Crocus olivieri*, and the blue *C. cancel-
latus*) and endemic fritillaries (*Fritillaria bythinica* and *F.
carica*), as well as the alpine squill, and the crimson-pink,
Gladiolus anatolicus. Of the mountains' interesting birds,
most are raptors—the short-toed eagle, long-legged and
honey buzzard, and the eagle owl; but there are colourful
presences to be seen in the woodland also, such as the
blue and red plumage of the rock thrush, with its characteristic white patch its back; and occasional sightings
of shearwaters (both Cory's and Yelkouan) are to be had
out to sea. One species of butterfly has its only European
home, high up at the tree-line on Mt. Ambelos; this is

the orange-banded hairstreak. The summit of Kerketéus is generally climbed from the south east in about three and a half hours each way: a rough, motorable track leads north from Votsalákia on the Gulf of Marathókambos, branches twice to the left and ends at the beginning of a footpath which climbs up to the convent of the Evangelístria (650m); from here a 90 minute climb brings you to Prophitis Elias (1,100m); the final ascent (45–60 minutes) reaches the summit of Vigla at 1,434m. From here, the meeting of Asia and Europe can be seen: in fact the peak you are standing on is an extinct volcano, which was brought into being by the slow collision of the Anatolian tectonic plate to the east, and the Eurasian plate to the north and west.

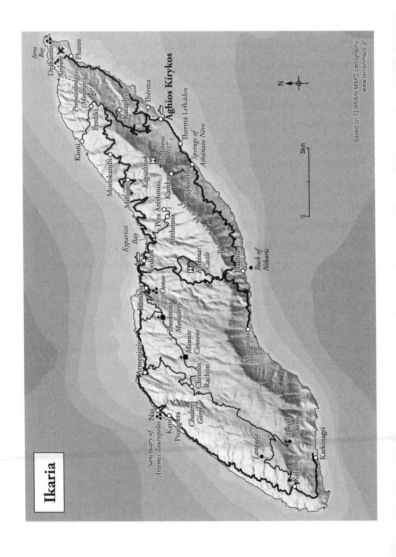

Ikaria

IKARIA

From any approach by sea, the island of Ikaría presents a forbidding wall of high mountains, steep slopes and rocky shores which—unprotected by any neighbouring land or island—bear the force of the winds from both north and south. Homer knew well the awful turbulence of the Ikarian Sea, to which he likened the mutability of mood in a crowd stirred by demagogy (*Iliad* II, 145): Horace, too, echoes its fearsome reputation at the very opening of his *Odes* (I.i.15–6). Once ashore, however, the island itself has a benign humanity: every village is an assemblage of fertile gardens, and its people seem bound by a deep sense of community. Tourism does not disturb here: it exists, but is a small element in a lively economy based primarily on cultivation. The Greeks, and the Ikarians themselves, joke about the island living in its own backwater of time; but the truth is that this very fact has served Ikaría well and made it a more congenial and unaffected island to visit than many.

Nothing quite prepares the visitor for the immense variety of landscapes: the high ridges of the east are densely clad in arbutus, heather and fern, and have the majesty of Scottish glens; some of the valleys and plateaux of the southwest, are wide, sandy and boulder-strewn as though they were parts of Colorado; gorges with water-falls and plane trees alternate with upland screes of improbably sculpted rock; there are forests of pine and of dwarf holm-oak; and however steep the gradient, it seems that every pocket that could be cultivated or terraced, has been. This is a volcanic landscape, and the evidence of the raw energy which formed it bubbles to the surface on the south coast where Ikaría's famous radioactive thermal springs have given both pleasure and therapeutic relief for well over two thousand years. Some of the springs are organised in spa establishments; others rise in the open by the sea.

The island has the remains of three ancient settlements, one of which, *Drakanon*, has a position and ruins which are superb and unforgettable. At the very opposite end of the island, the ancient port and sanctuary of Artemis *Tauropolos* at Nas is smaller and more intimate, but no less evocative. At the third, *Oenoe*, which was probably the island's largest settlement in Antiquity, a number of interesting buildings from Late Classical and Byzantine times have survived. All are, in different ways, unusual sites.

The unique fascination of Ikaría, though, is its 'wild west'—the western extremity of the island, into whose protected and beautiful interior the inhabitants retreated from the threat of piracy and invasion for long periods in recent history. Here can be found the strange troglodyte dwellings—half natural granite boulder, half stone-built house—which were used during these periods of retreat which have come to be known as 'the disappearances'. Here also are the *'Raches'* ('ridges'), the protected network of villages high above, where the life of this part of the island is centred and still follows its own idiosyncratic hours long into the night, as it was wont to do during 'the disappearances'. This area is, in many ways, the true heart of the island, for neither of the two main coastal towns, Aghios Kirykos and Evdilos, has the feel of an island *chora*.

Strange rocks, strange landscapes, strange waters, strange habits—at times, strange people—welcoming, unaffected, but idiosyncratic. Largely untrammelled by the less attractive aspects of modernity, Ikaría has preserved a particularly independent Greek identity—and a landscape that is equally rewarding for the naturalist, the rambler, the anthropologist, and the photographer.

HISTORY

That an island with such plentiful fresh water has been inhabited since early prehistoric times is no surprise. West of Aghios Kirykos, in the area of Glaredo, evidence of extensive Neolithic settlement has been found; and on the slopes to the west of the airport, at a locality known as Propezoulopi, a number of megaliths and menhirs are still to be seen *in situ*. From early in its history, it appears the island has had several names: '*Dolichi*' (elongated) and '*Ichtheoussa*' (rich in fish)—both accurate epithets. In fact the modern name 'Ikaría' is more likely to come from the Phoenician word for fish, '*ikor*', than from the mythical Icarus; the name may then have subsequently suggested itself by assonance as the location for the Icarus legends. The identity of Icarus in myth is typically variable and shows the superimposition of several stories (see below).

Ikaría is frequently cited in ancient literature, but nearly always—other than for the fable of Icarus—for the wildness of its seas, or for its famous Pramnian wine. Strabo's description is of an island with a virtually harbourless coast (*Geog.* XIV.1.19), and an interior mostly uninhabited except for a seasonal exploitation of its pasturage by the inhabitants of Samos (*Geog*, X.5.13). Two small Classical cities, *Oenoe* and *Therma*, were sufficiently established, however, to need to pay tribute separately to the Delian League. *Therma's* importance seems to have been superseded by the Hellenistic foundation of *Drakanon*, at the island's strategic eastern tip. Both *Therma* and *Oenoe* (whose importance must have been increased by the presence of the Sanctuary of Artemis *Tauropolos* in its territory) appear to have been further developed in Roman times, and *Oenoe* became the seat of the Byzantine governor.

The remains of the late 4th–5th century AD church of the Archangel at Miliopó show that Christianity was well established on the island relatively early. Under Byzantium, the island—now named 'Nikaria', and frequently used as a place of exile for unwelcome courtiers—was linked (as often before in Antiquity) to the destiny of Samos and Chios, passing together with them under the Genoese rule of the Zaccaria, and subsequently Arangio, families in the 14th and 15th centuries. In 1481 Ikaría was taken by the Knights of Rhodes as their most northerly possession, but fell to the Turks less than 40 years later in 1522. Throughout these uncertain centuries, in which the island was little protected and vulnerable to the predations of pirates, the inhabitants learned literally to disappear from sight into the invisible fastnesses of the mountains of the interior and to manage their own affairs for long periods which became known as the '*aphaineia*'—the 'disappearances'.

They perfected a kind of semi-asubterranean architecture, incorporating huge granite boulders *in situ* as the walls or roofs of dwellings, so as to be practically invisible from the sea. In this period, the remote valley of Langada in the southwest of the island became home of an unorthodox and autonomous administration. Although participating in the Independence Revolution of 1821, Ikaría did not go on to become part of the Greek State, and after 1835 fell back under Turkish rule. Finally, in 1912, in an almost bloodless revolution, the inhabitants evicted their Turkish overlords and with characteristic flair established an independent state of Ikaría, with its own constitution, flag (a white cross, centred in a blue background), postage stamps and anthem. Less than four months later it joined the free Greek State.

In the 20th century the island's population was depleted by wholesale emigration to the New World. During the Civil War of 1946–49, and later under the Colonels' Junta, Ikaría became once again a place of exile for political dissidents, who at times even outnumbered the inhabitants of the island. Mikis Theodorakis, the composer and musician, was exiled here in 1947. The island has a reputation for its vigorous left-wing political culture, and the presence of so many political exiles must have enforced, if not created, this tendency. This in turn has earned the island a measure of deliberate neglect by central government for long periods, reinforcing its natural self-reliance and independent pride. All this can still be readily sensed today, and helps constitute the island's unique character.

The guide to the island has been divided into three sections:-
- *Aghios Kírykos and the south coast of the island*
- *from Aghios Kírykos to Evdilos and Koskinás castle*
- *the west of the island from Kambos to Karkinágri.*

AGHIOS KIRYKOS AND THE SOUTH COAST OF THE ISLAND

(For distances, Aghios Kírykos = 0.0 km)

Aghios Kírykos—referred to locally just as 'Aghios'—is a pleasant and business-like port, named after the Eastern Church's youngest martyr (aged three) *(see pp. 155–56)*. Without being clearly centred around the sweep of a harbour-front, or gathered around a shaded *plateia*, or even grouped deferentially in the shadow of its principal church as island *choras* traditionally are, its centre is hard to locate. To the west it spreads into a grid of residential streets, dotted randomly with municipal buildings (the Demarcheion, the museum, etc.), and to the north its more functional quarter blends into other, older villages and settlements that climb the slopes of the mountain behind, and which partially occupy the site of the ancient settlement. The harbour itself is man-made, but it avails little in a strong southerly wind. The outer mole is dominated by a 7m tall bronze **monument to Icarus** erected by a local sculptor. It is difficult to know from which angle it is best to read this awkward piece, or what exactly it signifies. What remains of the old quarter of the town is to be found in a network of narrow streets just inland and west of the port.

The city's **Archaeological Museum** is currently closed for relocation (*T. 22750 24001 for information*). The jewel of the small collection is a fine early 5th century BC inscribed marble relief from Kataphygi by a certain 'Platthis' or 'Palion', depicting a family performing rituals before a seated deity nursing an infant.

THE SOUTH COAST, EAST OF AGHIOS KIRYKOS

Two kilometres east of Aghios Kírykos, the small settlement of **Thérma** lies at the foot of a steep and airless gorge, dotted with tamarisk and palm trees. Old-fashioned and a little frayed at the edges, this is a **thermal spa** frequented by Greeks from all over the country. The average age of the visitors is predictably high, but this means that it is possible to meet here with a rare and vanishing courtesy and at times eccentric cordiality, making it an unusual place to stay: both the landscape and its nature as a health spa, effectively cut the village off from the vulgar passage of time and the concerns of the rest of the world.

There are several springs at Thérma—'*Asklepios*', '*Apollon*', '*Artemis*', '*Pamphilis*' and '*Kratsas*'—but a number of them are now closed. All contain radium, in addition to a wide variety of mineral elements, and have been used mainly in the therapy of cardiovascular problems. They are also effective for rheumatic and arthritic conditions, and a variety of other disorders. The principal '*Apollon*' Spa opposite the shore (*open 7–1, 5–8*) provides 20-minute immersions in individual bath-tubs and cubicles, in which the hot water can be mixed with cold and the temperature regulated as desired. The water is clear and soft, but with a high salt content: its temperature is around 48°C and its radiation level high. It does not generally take long to feel its beneficent effects. The hot waters also flow out into the harbour, and their warmth can be felt in the water at places, while swimming.

These springs were well known in Antiquity and formed the nucleus of an ancient cure station and *Asklepeion*. Little remains to be seen in Therma itself, but by taking a path 400m east along the coast to **Chalasména Thérma**, the vestiges of a later Roman and early Byzantine thermal establishment can be seen. (*Take the path from east end of Therma bay, up to the Agriólykos Pension; pass through the terrace in front of the pension, up behind its far side and continue along a footpath for 10 minutes until it begins to descend to the rocky shore.*) Just before the path drops to the coast it passes (to right) a couple of chambers with small blind arches which formed part of the ancient thermal establishment. The masonry here would suggest an Early Byzantine date (c. 5th century AD); but the rock-cut channels and the square *piscina* of thermal water cut into the rock by the shore below, are probably much older. The complex was destroyed by earthquake, and never rebuilt.

The south east coast is largely empty and covered in low *maquis*. At 9.5km from Aghios Kírykos the road divides: left, to the island's small civil airport served now by almost daily flights to and from Athens; right to **Pharos**, a small, quiet coastal village with a pleasant shore-side taverna and a long **sandy beach**. One hundred metres before the road ends at the sea, at a poorly signed turning to the left, a track leads off to Ieros Bay and Drákanon. The last 500m of the footpath to the latter is heavily scented with myrtle: the path passes beside an unusual outcrop of rock—possibly once of ritual significance—with a flat face looking due east, and a minute cave underneath.

The ancient site of ***Drákanon** at the eastern extremity of the island is doubly impressive, both for its dramatic situation, and for the magnificent state of preservation of its Hellenistic tower, incorporated here into an enceinte of walls. The city guarded the Samos–Foúrni channel to the east, with Mount Kerketéus rising directly from sea to clouds in front of it; it also watched the main sea routes from Ephesus and upper Asia Minor to the Cyclades and western Aegean. The site offered a number of advantages for settlement: a natural rock acropolis on the north side, with a further summit and look-out post (controlling the western approach) directly behind and above (Mt. Vigla); two harbour inlets below, with two more distant anchorages and beaches for boats, both to the north (Ieros Bay), and south (Pharos Bay). It is known from inscriptions that the city of Drakanon was particularly associated with the cult of Dionysos—an important divinity on an island celebrated for its production of a prized wine.

The magnificently preserved 4th century BC *tower stands to nearly 30 courses of stone in height, and has no equals of its kind outside the tower at Aghios Petros on Andros. It would have survived in yet better condition had it not been used for naval target practice in the 19th century. Its blocks are of a visibly finer and more compact quality of marble than is found in the fortification walls of this site, and their faint bluish tinge would suggest that this might be marble brought from the Petrokopió quarry on Foúrni (*see p. 185*). The tower is constructed in exactly parallel courses, but with varying length and shape of block: each block is a perfect piece of craftsmanship, with concave rustication, drafted edges, and precisely dressed sides for snug fitting. The tower is entered by a beautifully arched doorway which faces due east. The interior is spacious, with a diameter of c. 6.5m. The fixing holes for two wooden floors can be seen clearly. What is particularly interesting in the case of this tower is its integration into the **system of fortifications**; it is situated at the narrow corner of a triangle of walls, the bases of whose bastions to north and south are also clearly visible. The **south bastion** is particularly well preserved with its internal entrance doorway still intact. Excavations are currently under way which are making the layout of the settlement clearer: they have also revealed to the east of the tower the foundations of several buildings, their thresholds visible as well as the bases of votive statues. A further excavation to the south, just within the walls, is bringing to light a hearth or altar base of the early Classical period, beside a small embrasure in the walls just south-east of the south bastion. A significant quantity of everyday objects, such as lamps and figurines, have been unearthed in the exca-vations.

A path leads down the hill to the east, through an area with a ground-cover of marble fragments and evidence of collapsed buildings, to the small **chapel of Aghios Gior-gios**, where a fluted antique altar has been incorporated into the interior wall of the apse. Further below are two natural, narrow harbours formed by projections of rock, whose sides show evidence of ancient port installations.

The only turning off the track between Drakanon and Pharos, skirts the airport runway and leads north to the

Bay of Ieros, a generally protected cove with a pleasant beach. A large **cave** in the hillside on the south side bears the evidence of ancient use. The whole inlet must have been an integral part of the Drakanon settlement, and used as a secondary harbour especially when the wind precluded use of the small harbours on the promontory.

THE SOUTH COAST, WEST OF AGHIOS KIRYKOS

Two kilometres south of Aghios Kírykos and 200m before a right turn to Glaredo, a tiny blue and white sign, reading 'Hot mineral springs', points down to the shore. The steep descent brings you to **Thermá Lefkádos**, where three very hot springs (c. 56–58°C), rich in iron and sulphur, rise below the rocks on the shore and mix to a pleasant temperature with the sea-water in a large pool roughly defined in the sea by a ring of boulders. The relatively high sulphur content makes these waters therapeutically indicated for dermatological conditions in particular. A further 1.5 km west along the coast road, the late 18th century **monastery of Lefkádos Evangelismós** stands above the road on the landward side. The *catholicon* is a finely proportioned compact structure: the apsidal cruciform plan, is surmounted first by a low, square crossing, and finally by an octagonal drum and shallow roof, constructed in traditional materials—creating a satisfying organic whole, both inside and out. The small complex is built on the site of a spring which originally fed a couple of **watermills** below. The remains of one is beside the road, and another on the cliff edge above the shore, clearly visible for its graceful arch which supports the water course and chute.

A little more than a kilometre beyond, just before entering the village of Xylosyrtis, a signed road leads down to the **springs of '*Athánato Neró*'** ('immortal water'), which rise at the shore—an excellent (cold) mineral water, with a light, metallic taste, very popular with locals who come here to collect it for use at table. **Xylosyrtis** itself (4.5km from Aghios Kírykos) is a delightful village of fertile gardens above a long shingle beach, stretching all the way to the handsome stone-built church of Aghia Paraskeví at its western end. In this area, the coastal strip varies between screes of barren rock, steep fertile valleys and patches of maquis; at Xylosyrtis, is the first outbreak of the huge, rounded, grey, granite boulders which characterise the landscape to the west of here at many points. At this point you are below the highest summit (1037m) of the massive ridge of Mount Athéras—the *Pramnos* of Antiquity.

At the western end of the village is a junction from which a road leads sharply back up the mountain to

Kamba—a *detour which is rewarding to make. The road is steep and climbs relentlessly, but affords marvellous views across the water towards Patmos and Astypalaia, with Donousa, Amorgos, and Naxos all visible on a clear day. The landscape is granitic, but there is occasional water giving rise to frequent outbreaks of green.

After 2km of climbing, the village of Kechritis comes into view on the right—an abandoned settlement, now ruined, of low stone houses which were deliberately designed to be almost indistinguishable from the rocky landscape. Above is the **church of Aghios Ioannis**, perched on a natural ledge where the rock itself constitutes the north wall of the narthex: inside is an iconostasis in local vernacular style. The road terminates at **Kamba**, a further kilometre and a half beyond, at a height of almost 700m above the shore which beetles below; above, the final rock wall of the summit rises a further 350m. There is a peaceful immensity to the view and the setting: the air is always clear and sharp. The simple, windowless, 18th century **church of the Panaghia**, constructed in un-rendered stone, although restored in 1965, still conserves its original roof of large schist slabs. Beyond it stretches a network of stone-walled fields bursting with vines. The special climate, altitude, humidity, soil and water on this almost alpine ledge favour the cultivation of a rich and excellent wine grape.

In Antiquity Ikaría was always renowned for its **Pramnian Wine**—an intense and very dark wine whose qualities must have required the grape to mature and reduce slowly in the colder autumnal temperatures of such an altitude. The vines here stand in a long line of descent from their prized, Pramnian ancestors.

PRAMNIAN WINE

It was into a concoction based on cheese, fresh honey and Pramnian wine, that Circe poured the potion which was to turn Odysseus's men into swine (*Od.* X. 635). In fact, Homer mentions the wine more than once, always indicating that it was mixed with grated cheese or barley: Plato, Aristophanes, Hippocrates, Diogenes Laertius and Athenaeus also describe or refer to it. But common to them all, is the suggestion that the wine was almost never drunk pure or for refreshment, but was most often used medicinally for its highly nutritive qualities. What can such a wine have been like? Athenaeus of Naucratis, the connoisseur of all matters of the palate, describes Pramnian wine thus (*Deipnosophistai*, I.15): 'it is a kind of wine that is neither sweet nor dense, but with a sharp and astringent and powerful taste' He goes on to relate how Aristophanes was wont to say that the effete Athenians never took any pleasure either in hard and steadfast poets, or in Pramnian wine, or indeed in anything difficult which might 'contract the stomach or cause a frown'. The wine was apparently 'black', was endowed with the 'power to assuage anger' and matured when left to stand (Hesychius of Alexandria). Eustathius, in his commentaries on Homer, says it was 'not for quenching thirst, but rather for alleviating satiety'—perhaps somewhat like a modern *digestif*. Hippocrates and Galen speak of its therapeutic qualities, both for external application as an unction (Hippocrates) and for internal consumption (Galen). Much later, the French Jesuit missionary, Jacques-Paul Babin, again described the wine as 'hard', but added that the island had 'the best winter grapes I ever encountered, being round and red, and growing between the rocks in such dangerous places that they are gathered with considerable hazard'. (The same Fr. Babin was astonished to note that the islanders of Ikaría rowed their boats naked, explaining to him that clothes were an impediment to them and wore out too quickly when rowing.)

It is hard to find anything today on Ikaría that corresponds to this impressive variety of qualities and descriptions: indeed it would be unusual for such a type of wine to have remained unchanged throughout so many centuries. Interestingly, however, the use of a warm drink of red wine heated with barley in it can still be found in winter among the older rural inhabitants, both here and on Samos. It remains only to experiment with adding grated sheep's cheese to find something that might possibly have seemed familiar to Odysseus.

Back on the principal coast road, the villages that follow to the west of Xylosyrtis—**Chrysóstomos** (8km), Valanidiá (9km), Vróni (10km), **Plaghiá** (14km)—are dotted with schist-tiled stone houses, and immersed in a landscape of olives, cypresses, pomegranates, figs and occasional monumental Aleppo pines. A number of freshwater springs rise in this area and fill the narrow gorges that run down to the shore. As the road rises, ruined walls, farmsteads and disused threshing circles can be seen below on the rise above the shore. From Vroni, a small trapezoid-shaped rock is visible in the bay just off-shore: this is the **rock of *Nikaris***—so named, because it traditionally marks the place where Icarus fell into the sea and drowned on his airborne escape from Crete.

THE LEGEND OF ICARUS

Although the pictorial image of a mythical human flight may appear on vase-painting much earlier, the literary accounts of the escape of Daedalus and Icarus from the Labyrinth of Crete are all surprisingly late: we have nothing earlier than the end of the 1st century BC. Ovid's account in the *Metamorphoses* (VIII 182 ff) is the fullest, and it is closely related to that in Hyginus's *Fabulae*. An older version of the story, however, is probably represented by that recounted in Pausanias (*Description of Greece*, IX.11) in which Daedalus whom King Minos of Crete had imprisoned together with his son Icarus in the Labyrinth (designed by Daedalus himself at Minos's command), escapes not by airborne flight, but by a boat rigged with his newly-invented sails which were able to outrun the oar-powered ships of Minos. Daedalus fared well, but Icarus who did not properly understand how to control his sails, capsized and drowned in the sea near *Lebinthos* (Levitha, 40km west of Kalymnos). His body was washed by the storm to Ikaría where, in other accounts, it was later found and buried by Hercules. Ovid's version—more romantic and far better known—has the ingenious Daedalus make wings of wax and feathers for the escape. Before embarking Daedalus advises his son, in model Greek fashion, to fly always at a *reasonable* level, neither too low, where humidity might weigh down the feathers, nor too high where the sun might melt the binding wax. Once well out of danger, Icarus began in a natural and understandable delight in being airborne to fly higher and higher, provoking the inevitable consequences foreseen by his father. Calling out to his father, Icarus falls into the sea and drowns, leaving Daedalus to bury his son's body ashore on the island which, as Ovid says, has ever since conserved his name. Ovid's account is vivid and moving: its details inspired Breughel's masterpiece of 1569, *Landscape with the Fall of Icarus*; and the painting in turn inspired W.H. Auden's beautiful poem, written around 1932, '*Musée des Beaux Arts, Brussels*' (where the picture is still to be seen).

Beyond Plaghiá the land becomes more arid and the road rises rapidly into a wide natural amphitheatre of cliffs. At 18.5km the road branches, with the main road (a dramatic and beautiful alternative route) continuing up over the summit in the direction of Evdilos. The left branch drops down steeply towards the coast, passes through a 500m tunnel, recently blasted through the cliffs, and on to **Manganitis** (25km), in an isolated and astonishing **landscape of vast granite boulders**—round, egg-shaped, or variedly sculptural in form. Houses lurk next to boulders larger than themselves, gardens skirt around others that appear to have been dropped into them, and the whole area is filled out with abundant Aleppo pines. Today, Manganitis is largely a quiet, recreational spot with a couple of good *mezedopoleia*, and an attractive and tiny harbour. The road ends here and a track continues a further 2km to the isolated church of Aghios Nektarios, perched between 800m of granite cliff and the sea.

FROM AGHIOS KIRYKOS TO EVDILOS AND KOSKINAS CASTLE

(For distances, Aghios Kírykos = 0.0km)

The road north from Aghios Kírykos climbs tortuously through a number of almost contiguous villages. The valley through which it winds was once both more watered with springs and more forested with trees—at several point **ruined watermills** can be seen, some still in relatively good state of preservation; of the tree cover which until recently clad these slopes, the solitary white **Monument to the Victims of the Forest Fires** of 1993 on the open scree to the west of Kountoumas is the most poignant reminder. (*The monument is reached by a long winding track and a final flight of steps, off from the main road.*) The landscape to the east of the road is gentler, and intensively cultivated—the older houses and farmsteads recognisable by their silver-grey, schist-tile roofs. From Mavráto (7.5km) a path leads steeply west towards the summit of the ridge (45 minutes) to the remains of **Kapsalinokastro**, a 15th century fortress, wedged in the rocks on the ridge with ample **views** of the surrounding waters to north, east and south.

At 10.1km, after the scattered, agricultural centres of Mavrikato and Oxea with their wide panoramic sites, a road drops sharply off to the left to **Kataphygi** on the slopes below. The villages in this area have many stone houses dating from the last 200 years: the church and adjacent school house are both fine buildings from the same period. Due south a hill rises to a summit of 470m: this was the site of the **Archaic settlement of *Kataphydion*,** which was used through and beyond Classical times as the acropolis for *Therma*, on the coast below. It is hard to make much sense of the lay-out of the site, since all that remain are quantities of collapsed masonry along the summit; some remnants of the lower courses of the citadel walls are discernible, however, on the edge of the south escarpment of the hill.

A kilometre beyond the Kataphygi turning, the main Aghios Kírykos–Evdilos road reaches its **summit** (11km from Aghios Kírykos) beside a small military station and wind farm, from where there are commanding views of the islands of Foúrni and Samos.

A detour to the north

The attractive and traditional village of **Perdikí**, lies below and to the north of here, 2km down the branch road to the north: it has many fine, stone houses, and a small Folklore Museum, densely packed with examples of earthenware and ceramic pottery, woodwork, tools and implements, both agricultural and domestic. The unpaved road out of the village's eastern extremity skirts (after 1.5km) the castle of Kefalas, passes the abandoned settlement of Aghios Savvas, and, before dropping to sea level at the airport, descends the hill of **Propezoúlopi**, where a number of **prehistoric menhirs** can still be seen in the adjacent fields. Turning left to the shore, just before the airport, will bring you to the bay of Aghia Kyriakí, where there are hot springs rising in the small enclosure below the overhang of rock to the left. From the western end of Perdikí, a paved road leads down (4.7km) to the coast at **Kioni**, where there are the remains of an Early Christian **church of Aghios Giorgios**.

Back on the main road, after the wind-farm the road turns sharply west into a very different landscape of deeply folded ravines—wilder, more deserted and dense-ly covered with heather, fern and low arbutus. The first signs of habitation are at Monokámbi (16.5km), a tiny and formerly very isolated settlement in a dense break of vegetation—olive, pine, chestnut, cypress and ilex— completely hidden from sight from the sea below. Visible from the road to the north of the village, and dwarfed by a ridge of slanting schist rock, is the tiny, **rock-cut chapel of Aghia Sophia** (*access by path and steps from north end of village*). These hidden villages have many early 18th century churches, with traditional schist-tile roofs, white-washed outside and mostly undecorated inside. After Ploúmari (18.5km) the road skirts a wide gorge. At 21km, before the road turns sharp west and back into the next ravine, a stone path leads from the roadside up on to the ridge above, beside the rudimentary and ancient **church of Aghia Ioulitta and Aghios Kírykos**. Saints Julitta and Kírykos, from Iconium in Asia Minor (modern Konya), were mother and infant son: Kirykos was killed in Tarsus, during the persecutions of Diocletian, at the age of three, and his mother was later beheaded in 296. The building is hard to date because its roof has been rebuilt and an incongruous column added to support it; but the simple flagstone floor and roughly assembled walls may be of considerable antiquity. There are remains of fortifications, cisterns and habitations on the spur of Gerakas above and to the north—and magnificent views in all directions. Just beyond, in the next ravine, below the tiny settlement of Miliopó (22 km) are the interesting remains of the **Early Christian basilica of the Taxiarchis**. This is perhaps the island's earliest surviving place of Christian worship.

From Miliopó, through the area of Karavóstamo (29.5km), and down to the coast at Evdilos (36.5km), the road weaves repeatedly inland and then back towards the sea, as it skirts ravine after ravine, slowly descending through a terrain that becomes less inimical and ever more cultivated. The settlements are mostly modern: their predecessors, from the period of the *'aphaineia'* or 'disappearances' (*see History above*), are all higher up inland so as to be protected from coastal piracy. One such village (4km south from the junction at Kiparisi bay) is **Aréthousa**: separated from Evdilos by only a few kilometres, but by as many decades in time, it still maintains some of the characteristics of rural life which have been lost elsewhere in Greece. It is a loose group of scattered villages—**Pera Aréthousa**, the remotest of them, is now no more than a collection of abandoned stone dwellings. Life centres around the vines, the cultivating of fruits (especially apricots and plums) and the production of cheeses. Even *kafeneia* are few and far between: but in them can often be found intense and old-style local wines—together with some equally intense and old-style political commentaries and a sense of dress and décor that has remained unchanged for a lifetime.

At the central point of the north coast, **Evdilos** (36.5km), meaning 'clear' or 'visible', is the capital of the north of the island—a peaceful, attractive and unaffected port on the route from Piraeus to Samos, with an old quarter on the hill to the west directly above the harbour. In Antiquity Evdilos, whose name was *Histoi*, may have functioned as a subsidiary commercial port to the main, Classical settlement on the north coast, *Oenoe* (modern Kambos), 2.5km to its west. The deep, fertile, protected valley which cuts across the island to its south was the island's principal granary and source of wealth. It therefore needed protection, and this was provided throughout the Middle Ages by the impressively sited **castle of Koskinás*, which was at the centre of a network of further outlying castles (Kapsalinokastro, Gerakas and Kefalas below Perdikí, which have been mentioned above). (*The castle is 8.5km due south of Evdilos, to the east of the road which connects it with Plaghiá on the south coast. Five kilometres from Evdilos, at Akamatra, an unmetalled road leads off towards the castle. Alternatively, an equally dramatic approach can be made from the south from the Plaghiá road, where 800m after the summit of the ridge, an unmetalled road leads 3.5km to the castle which soon appears on its conical peak above the wide granite landscape. The rusting iron tower for winching up materials during restoration works on the site is visible from afar.*) The castle, whose walls are in relatively good state of preservation, perches precariously at an altitude of over 700m, and is entered by a small, low gate in the enceinte. The bases of two watch-towers (to NW and SE) are clearly visible. The construction is originally Byzantine, dating from the 11th or 12th century, and must have been adopted and partially modified with the arrival of the Genoese overlords in the 14th century, who probably then rebuilt the large **church of Aghios Giorgios Dorganás** ('St. George of the Shining Spear') which dominates the summit. The austere, un-rendered stone interior of the church contains a number of ancient *spolia*: a granite column in its *templon* screen, and a finely fluted drum which supports the altar. Also clearly visible here, incorporated into the body of the south and west walls, and the corners of the sanctuary, are a number of **immured clay pots**: this was an ancient Byzantine habit which enhanced the acoustics of a building for chanted liturgy. Although the views over the island from here are vast, the peak of Kefálas just to the north inconveniently hides Chios from view, and to the south east, Naxos is similarly hidden. However visibility is good from here to the other castles on Ikaría—amongst which are those better situated for chain-signalling through the islands. The purpose of this castle must therefore have been more for surveillance and protection of the rich agricultural valleys and inhabited areas of the interior. The land may seem barren today, but the immaculate and extensive **network of walls, bridges and stone paths** in the gorge below at Kosíkia to the west of the castle is testimony to the formerly dense cultivation in this valley.

THE WEST OF THE ISLAND —
KAMBOS TO KARKINAGRI

(For distances, Kambos = 0.0 km)

Around the bay and village of Kambos (2.5km west of Evdilos) are the remains of **ancient** *Oenoe*, whose name, cognate with the Greek word for 'wine', is a clue to the source of its wealth and the reason of its fame. The site is a very clear choice for an early settlement: a natural acropolis dominating a fertile estuary, and a beach and port for boats. The shoreline will have retreated considerably in 2,000 years through the silting up of what was probably a harbour inlet which reached some way inland along the east side of the acropolis hill. The wine—some of it the Pramnian wine mentioned above—produced on the slopes of the valleys to the south, would have been traded and exported through the port and city on this site. Prosperity from the wine trade will, in turn, have made the city an obvious choice of seat for later Roman and Byzantine governors; and it is the evidence of their presence that remains today, clearly visible as you descend on the road from Evdilos. Referred to locally as '**Palatia**', the ruined complex, with conspicuous arched windows, visible on the northeast side of the acropolis hill in the centre of the valley, is the principal remnant of what was probably a Byzantine governor's residence created out of a variety of earlier Roman buildings. (*Access is easiest from around the western side of the hill.*) Though officially referred to as a **Roman odeion**, the construction method and masonry would indicate something very late if it were Roman—more probably 5th or 6th century AD, and therefore Early Byzantine. The design, furthermore, with an unusually wide and shallow *cavea* and scarcely much space for performers, does not preclude the building's use as an *odeion* (an intimate auditorium for concerts or recitals), but suggests that it might more likely have been an audience chamber for the local governor. The window arches and the blind arcade behind the *cavea* (whose purpose must have been decorative) are beautifully constructed in clear white marble from Foúrni, while the external quoins have been recently replaced in white concrete. The summit of the acropolis above reveals the base of a fortress tower, but little else of substance beyond the fine views.

Completely hidden out of sight from the sea, and set below the summit of the hill on the south side, is the fine 12th century **church of Aghia Irini**, built over part of the site of a much larger **5th century basilica**, vestiges of whose once magnificent **mosaic flooring** are visible on the north side of the area in front of the entrance of the church and beneath the steps which lead to the museum above. The mosaics are executed in five colours (two blues, white, red and yellow): various geometric and 'knot' designs, and ivy-leaf border motifs. Sunk into the ground in front of the southwest corner of the church is an ancient sarcophagus—smaller, but similar in design, to the fine example in the *plateia* of Foúrni (*see p. 179*). The 5th century basilica must have been a large building, stretching from just beyond the apse of the present church (where the Early Christian foundations are just visible) as far west as the rather odd monumental gateway and belfry which opens onto the area before the façade of the existing church. This **gateway** is a more recent assemblage of ancient marble *spolia* from the site, designed principally to house the church's bell. Countless other *spolia*, both Classical and Early Christian, plain and inscribed, lie all around or are incorporated wholesale into the older houses and buildings of the area. The interior of the existing, 12th century church of Aghia Irini, surmounted by a high octagonal dome, has an unusual **synthronon** at its east end—a memory perhaps of its Early Christian predecessor. The paintings that once covered its walls may well lie beneath the whitewash: some, in very poor condition, are just visible under an arch in the northeast corner. Interestingly they appear to be an-iconic: this may indicate that the 12th structure incorporates part of the Early Christian basilica here.

Just above the church is the small **museum** *(no regular opening times, outside morning openings in the summer months: the knowledgeable supervisor, Vassilis (T. 22750 31300), who holds the key, runs the café and shop on the main road just below and is always willing to open the collection on request).* The collection contains finds from all round the north of the island, not just from *Oenoe*: a small number of interesting Neolithic pieces; fragments of pottery; some eroded marble statuettes from Nas; an unusual **marble fragment with Dionysiac ivy-leaf motif**; many **inscriptions**, including one (Hellenistic) declaiming Ikarians as liars, in which the word 'Ikarians' has been substituted by 'Jews' probably in Roman times. (A number of newer and more interesting finds are currently being cleaned and documented in the Archaeology Department workshop, two doors up from the café/shop on the main road: it is worth asking to see inside, if the door should be open.)

THE COAST: FROM KAMBOS TO ARMENISTÍS (DIRECT)

(Kambos = 0.0km)

After Kambos, the main road runs due west following the line of the shore. Beside the first sharp bend above the western side of the Kambos valley is the minuscule and ancient **church of Aghia Sophia** (1km), overlooking the sea. Its roof is in local schist tiles, and its low doorway constructed of marble spolia from nearby *Oenoe*. The coastline beyond offers many amenities for the visitor and holidaymaker: the stretch between Gialiskári and Armenistís, bordering two contiguous and beautiful **sandy beaches**, constitutes Ikaría's principal tourist resort. **Armenistís** (9.5km) has a number of travel services, tavernas, and the widest variety of good hotels on the island. It is an attractive, and still little-developed village. The surrounding landscape has been badly damaged by forest fires in recent years, but is slowly re-foresting in areas.

THE INTERIOR: FROM KAMBOS TO CHRISTÓS RACHÓN

(Kambos = 0.0km)

From the western side of the Kambos inlet, a beautiful route climbs southwest through the hills to the **Theoktístis** Monastery** (6km), immersed in trees and heavily scented air (*visiting hours 8–1, 4–8*). In origin this was a hermitic settlement, out of sight of the world, with a number of caves for dwellings, hollowed out from under the huge natural monoliths that punctuate the landscape in this area. The appearance of these dwellings is remarkably similar to some in Cappadocia, in central Anatolia—an area with which the original hermits here may well have had contact. Today there is only one resident monk. The *catholicon* is a small vaulted building, heavily buttressed at its western end. It is remarkable for the 17th century cycle of **wall-paintings** in its interior which, though over-cleaned in the past, is almost complete and reveals an unusually sophisticated style. Of particular interest are: the *Baptism of Christ* in a River Jordan teeming with fish—one particularly large one by his foot—playing on the Christological symbolism of fish (*south side of ceiling*); the panels depicting the dominating presence of the *Archangels*, and of *St George with the Dragon*; and a

dramatic *Christ and the Harrowing of Hell* and the raising of Adam, Eve and good pagan souls from Limbo. The
style is sophisticated and confident, full of vigour and
clarity of design, indicating that this painter was no local,
vernacular artist. Directly behind the outside of the east
end of the church is a cramped, **rock-cut hermit's sleep-
ing cell**; another is at the foot of the steps to the south of
the monastery area; and the largest—and most dramatically troglodytic of all—at the top of the flight of steps,
sandwiched below a projecting granite boulder of prepos-
terous dimensions. The hermit's 'lair' has been walled in
and converted into a simple chapel, embellished with a
pleasingly painted wooden screen. In icons and in Early
Christian thinking, a cave symbolises man's ignorant and
unenlightened condition in this world, as he waits upon
the illumination of the Divine: in the daily cycle of hermitic life, the hermit returns each night into its darkness,
so as to be able newly to rejoice in the redeeming light of
the following dawn—the symbol of divine enlightenment.

In the village of **Pigí** (6.5km) just above the monastery are two stone-roofed churches side by side, typical of
so many in the area—simple, unpainted, vaulted spaces,
with occasionally some ancient or Byzantine *spolia* incorporated into the fabric, as is the case here in the lower
of the two churches, dedicated to Aghios Ioannis The-

ologos. From Máratho (7.5km) to the **monastery of the Annunciation** ('*Moní Monté*') (12.3 km) the road winds through woods of pine and *ilex*, chestnut and oak, interspersed with rock boulders on the sandy floor. The monastery feels institutional after the spontaneity of Theoktístis; its more modern buildings (19th century) are the immaculate home of a small community of nuns. There is great tranquility in its shaded setting and its courtyard where it is possible to have refreshments. Shortly beyond, the road passes across a small and picturesque **artificial lake**, created for water conservation and now home to a variety of resident and migrating birds.

Spread across a wide hollow between rugged hills, **Ráches** ('ridges') is in effect a collection of several contiguous villages; its principal centre, '**Christós Rachón**' (16.5km), is an unexpected pleasure to come upon, however—lush, peaceful, hidden away and difficult to perceive as a whole, because its seemingly endless tissue of tiny houses immersed each in its own garden is soon lost in the dense vegetation. Bustling with life, especially when the young emerge from school into its tiny centre of stone-paved streets shaded by pergolas or trees and lined with cafés and tavernas, Christós has long been the commercial centre of this part of the island, in particular during the periods of the 'disappearances'. It is still the heart of the west of the island today—a large and relaxed community of prospering villagers who, being used to managing their own affairs for long periods, have acquired an eccentric independence of language, manners and time and a pleasing insouciance towards the rest of the world. The 'outside' world seems unusually far away here.

Ráches is the heart of an area which is well-suited for walking: information and maps for suggested routes are available in Christós Rachón, in the photography and stationery shops.

*Detour to Aghios Isidoros, Langada and Kalamos
(For distances, Kambos = 0.0 km)
It is beyond Ráches to the south that the unforgettable character of western Ikaría is most to be felt. There is a good, but un-metalled, road which passes through Karydies (17.5km), climbs onto the plateau of Stravokountoura, passes Pezi (23.5km), Aghios Isidoros (27km), descends to Langada (30.5km), and eventually finishes on the south coast at Karkinágri (40km). *It is one of the more varied and memorable and dramatic stretches of road in the Aegean. (*The return can be made to Armenistís by the coast road, as per the last section below in reverse order.*)

From Ráches the road heads due south through the

walnut groves of Karydiés. 1.5km west of Karydiés, the asphalt ends at a junction (19km): from here the left branch climbs steeply south through pine-woods onto a plateau where the road runs beside an artificial water reservoir. The wide, shallow valley to the south of the reservoir, is at first fertile and green, but bordered by ridges of pure rock; by the time you reach the signposted junction for Aghios Isidoros (25.5km), the landscape has already become a sandy, boulder-strewn desert. The short detour (1.3km) from here to Aghios Isidoros leads over the watershed and drops down on the southern face of the ridge, through woods of miniature *ilex* trees to the solitary **church and spring of Aghios Isidoros** (once a hermitage), looking out at immense height over a balcony of improbably shaped rocks to the sea. There is a taverna here—surely one of the boldest places imaginable to have a taverna: it opens only in the summer, and bursts into life naturally at the feast of Aghios Isidoros on 14 May, when this remote spot is transformed by crowds of local pilgrims. After returning again to the junction, the road climbs over a barren rocky plateau to the watershed; just beyond, it bursts upon the densely green and watered **valley of *Langada** (27km). This wide and beautiful upland valley is completely cut off and invisible from the sea—hence its choice as the principal retreat during the 'disappearances' of the 15th to 18th centuries, when the local inhabitants withdrew from proximity to the coast to avoid pirate raids, and established self-governing and undisturbed communities in places such as this. Langada was the principal among these, and was the seat of the islanders' self-appointed council and chief: the **abandoned municipal buildings** from this period are still to be seen at the northeastern end of the valley. Some sense of Langada's importance as a capital is given by the impressive **church of the Panaghitsa**, at the base of the valley amidst a grove of immense and ancient plane-trees. The numerous ranks of stone tables and seats below these giant planes scarcely accommodate all the visitors who come here for the interminable eating, drinking and dancing during the island's greatest *panegyri* for the Feast of the Virgin (14–16 August). The feast's importance—and the significance of this almost deserted place of Langada—is still deeply felt by the islanders.

After Langada, the road climbs once more, now in sight of the sea, traverses a ridge of massive boulders and descends sharply, passing the picturesque and abandoned **stone farmhouses of Kalamos** (34km). These scattered buildings, hidden and shaded by pines, which blend perfectly with the rocky cliff face are amongst the best examples of the island's vernacular architecture—well-proportioned, securely built and, in materials and design, at one with the landscape. Below Kalamos the road joins the coastal route from Armenistís to Karkinágri — subject of the next section.

ARMENISTIS TO KARKINAGRI

(For distances, Armesistís = 0.0 km)
(The road along Ikaría's west coast is un-metalled, but passable for all vehicles. It is 27km from Armensitís to Karkinágri. There are no filling stations.)

Three-and-a-half kilometres south west along the coast road from Armenistís is Kato Ráches, the 'window' and coastal stepping-off place for Ráches in the upland interior: the two were linked by 4–5km of steep paths and mule-tracks which followed and skirted the **Chálari Gorge** which debouches into the sea at this point. The marked paths that follow and traverse the gorge are fascinating for the naturalist and rewarding for the rambler. The gorge is a succession of pools and cascades, and its protected micro-climate has encouraged a varied and interesting **flora and fauna**. There are several varieties of cyclamen and wild orchid. The kingfisher is a regular resident here, most easily observed in winter when the trees are bare; little egrets are common in the lower reaches, and the characteristic sharp call of the little owl and the melancholy bleep of the Scops owl can often be heard in the inland areas in the evening. Rare migrants include the black-winged stilt, and little bittern.

Such a densely wooded gorge was, in Antiquity, the natural domain of the huntress goddess, Artemis. The Chalaris river would at that time have carried much more water and its small estuary would have formed the only viable roadstead for boats on the west side of the island. Above this natural harbour, therefore, the *Sanctuary of Artemis Tauropolos** at Nas grew up. ('*Tavropolos*' means 'drawn by a yoke of bulls' or perhaps 'hunting bulls'; 'Nas' is a corruption of '*naos*', 'a temple'). This seemingly re-mote spot had great importance in Antiquity as the first or last harbour on the Asia Minor side of the Aegean for pilgrims on their way to or from the Sanctuary of Apollo on Delos. (Delos was also the birthplace of Artemis.) The longest and most exposed stretch of the sea-journey was between here and Mykonos. The popularity of the cult of Artemis spread from Asia Minor (principally Ephe-sus), and this sanctuary, established already by the 7th century BC, would appear to be one of the oldest in the Greek Islands. Clement of Alexandria (*Protrep*. IV.46) mentions that the cult statue of the goddess here was not only 'wooden', but 'unworked'—implying that (like the original image of Hera on Samos) it was a sacred piece of natural wood which was in some way suggestive of the image and presence of the goddess, without the profaning intervention of the hand of man.

The site of **Nas** is tranquil and beautiful, but little of substance remains to be seen: the columns and statuary, which were recorded as being still visible on the site a little over a hundred years ago, were later zealously consigned to the kilns to make mortar for new churches in the area. The site banks up the hill to the south side of the river inlet, now closed by a sandbar. At the lowest level are the remains of some late 1st century BC **wharfs** and constructions for the port and boats; just above, the main terrace has a heterogeneous group of foundations, in a variety of different materials. The long, rectangular, stepped construction in yellow–brown sandstone, though west-facing, has the appearance of an **altar**: beside it is a small rectangular base in grey granite with four precise perforations possibly for the railing protecting a sacred image. Further up, there is extensive terracing which, at several points, has been rebuilt in later times. Above all of this, and perfectly oriented to the cardinal points, is a **podium**, about 26m on its longer north–south axis, on which the principal temple may have been erected. Beyond this point, the litter of potsherds on the southern hillside is witness to the extent and density of habitation here. The site, especially towards sunset, has a pure and austere beauty appropriate to Artemis.

Beyond Nas is the tiny settlement of **Kato Proespéra** (6km): 3km uphill to the south of it, on the left-hand branch road, is Ano Proespéra where **burials** from Geometric through to Roman times have been excavated and documented. Along the road between the two villages can be seen many of the extraordinary *'**invisible' dwellings**, used during the 'disappearances'. The landscape is dotted with massive, naturally smoothed, granite boulders: often on the landward side of such a rock, invisible from the sea, a rudimentary house has been constructed in stone up against, and under the lea of, the boulder. In other instances, the small gap between a group of close rocks may have been roofed over with stone tiles to create a dwelling, again completely un-discernible from a distance. Many of these dwellings are of considerable antiquity—up to 500 and 600 years old in some cases. Seeking them out, however, is like spotting well camouflaged birds.

Along the west coast, the few villages—mere clusters of old stone houses—are generally grouped around a small church beside a spring or torrent. At the lower levels they are tiny; higher up the slopes they are set back from sight and are larger. At **Mavrianó** (14.5km), the 18th century **monastery church of the Panaghia Evangelistrias** surprises by its size and position overlooking the shore. Here the handsome octagonal drum and schist-tiled cupola are above the narthex, rather than the crossing. The low monastery buildings enclose the *catholicon* compactly. As so often, there is the tell-tale presence of some ancient spolia in the enclosure.

At Kálamos (21.5km) the coast road joins with the route from Christós Rachón and Langada (*see previous detour itinerary*). The last 6km of road (now metalled) round the point of Cape Papas and descend into the narrow, fertile coastal plain of **Karkinágri** (27km). Only a few of the old stone houses remain from the time when Karkinágri was an isolated fishing port; it is now a place of summer retreat and recreation, with a couple of good tavernas and a sprinkling of modern houses and gardens hemmed between the mountains, facing to the sea and the sun in the south. A caïque service runs between Karkinágri and Aghios Kírykos three times a week in good weather (typically Mon, Wed and Fri). The journey along the wild and precipitous south coast of the island leaves a vivid impression of the island's geography.

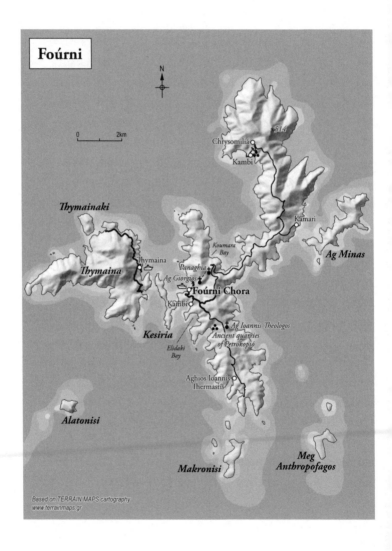

FOURNI

Foúrni is an archipelago of several islands south of the channel that separates Ikaría from Samos, of which only the two largest—Foúrni and Thýmaina—are properly inhabited. Strabo had rightly called Ikaría '*alimenos*', or 'harbourless': but Foúrni, its neighbour, is the very opposite. Its several islands protect one another from the winds, and their coasts are so heavily indented that there is any number of natural harbours. These coastal waters have always been remarkably rich in fish, and the island's economy is based almost solely on its fishing-fleet. Its plentiful catches (predominantly lobster and red mullet) are shipped to Piraeus. The land, however, is in no way as rich as the water, having been almost entirely deforested over a century ago by charcoal burners, leaving a sharp profile of hills and a largely bare shoreline at the sea. The modern name, Foúrni, meaning 'the furnaces' probably derives from this large-scale charcoal production.

In Antiquity the island's name was *Korsiai*, and its fame rested on the quality of its superb marble. One of the best preserved ancient marble quarries in the Aegean is in Petrokopió Bay, where many well-formed architectural elements in pure white marble still lie discarded by the shore awaiting a delivery journey that never materialised. The quality of the stone, remarkably free of veins and faults, was so good both for building and for sculpture that it was widely used on Ikaría and Samos, and at Ephesus in Asia Minor, as well as further afield.

Today the island is a pleasant and quiet retreat, with a delightful *chora* and attractive *plateia* at its centre, and a waterfront where good, fresh fish and lobster can often be enjoyed from the same day's catch. Foúrni is best visited in the spring when it is a carpet of minuscule wild flowers: or else, after a long dry summer, when the first rains come in September and the whole atmosphere of the archipelago lifts with what seems like the scent of honey.

✳ ✳ ✳ ✳ ✳

The modern **Chora** of Foúrni is pleasingly grouped in a theatre-shaped ring of hills, and occupies a small fertile plain watered by the confluence of several seasonal torrents. It has two beautiful and memorable characteristics: the straight, marble-paved main street lined with mulberry trees which leads straight up from the port, and on which the evening *volta* takes place; and the charming **main square** to which it leads, shaded with planes and ringed round with *kafeneia* and several old, stone houses. One corner of the square is dominated by a massive (lidless) ancient **carved sarcophagus of the Roman period** (1st century AD), of local marble, which was found on the edge of the town in the area of the Roman cemetery. Its sides are decorated with a design found widely in Asia Minor and which is generally typical of Ionian Greece and of Greek Egypt: the rings and pendants, which normally have the form of carved garlands of leaves with hanging bunches of grapes, are here completely undefined, so also the rosettes in the centre of the swags. This is not because the piece is unfinished (the surface would be rough if this were the case), but because such a stylised and reduced form of the traditional iconographic elements was fashionable in certain periods and situations, not least because it was a considerably less expensive solution. On the sarcophagus's north side the inscribed epitaph is visible of '*Epameinon, son of Telon and Philte*', who died at the age of 25. The inside shows clearly the chisel and running-drill marks left from the hollowing out of the block, instructive of the methods used by the stone-cutters for such a process. Across the square, is the main church of the island, dedicated to Aghios Nikolaos; like nearly all of the other churches and most of the town, it was built within the last 70 years. A few decaying stone houses of an earlier epoch still stand at the foot of hill behind the *plateia*.

The *chora* of Foúrni lies over the site of the ancient

settlement, whose acropolis was above on the top of the sharp spur directly to the northeast. The points of greatest historical interest are to be found on this ring of projecting summits above the town. They are best reached by taking the principal road (surfaced only for the first 2km) which leaves from the south, but circles round above the town before heading north. As the road at first climbs from the harbour to the south, it passes below the church and cemetery of Aghia Triada on the left. On the saddle above (1km) are four restored windmills, which mark the descent on the southern side into **Kambí** and its bay. Kambí is no more than a cluster of gardened houses, and a couple of seasonal tavernas beside an attractive and sheltered beach and harbour. At 1.7km is a junction: the road to the left heads north to Chrysomiliá (15km), to the right it continues south to Aghios Ioannis Thermastís (6km).

NORTH TO CHRYSOMILIA

Seven hundred metres beyond the junction the asphalt ends; after a further 500m, on the left just above the road as it flattens out at the summit, is the **church of Aghia Marina** (also reached directly by a very steep path—easier to follow on the descent than on the way up—from behind the *plateia*), in a panoramic setting amongst pines and cypress on the crest of the ridge. A few remains—**columns**, **capitals** and **marble *templon* screen elements**—gathered together at the side of the church are testimony to a Byzantine predecessor.

Five hundred metres further northwards, you pass the modern church of Aghia Irini Chrysovalandou to the right, and, just as the road descends, the **church of the Panaghia** comes into sight on another narrow ridge with ample views both down to the town and north to Chrysomiliá from its attractive and shaded precinct. Visible from here towards the southwest, on a lower ridge, and reached by a rough path (15 minutes), is the **chapel of Aghios Giorgios** built on the summit of a spur which served as a small ancient acropolis for Foúrni, which may not have been more than a large defensive fort. There is visible evidence of ancient construction in the form of cut and drafted blocks and eroded architectural elements lying to the east of the church. The position dominates the whole of the bay below and represents an ideal site for a fortress and garrison.

To the west of the front of the modern church of Aghios Giorgios is a curious triangular cut made in the living rock, a little over 2m in length along it base. There are graffiti, ancient and modern, in the area: one ancient inscription reads, '*Longing for offspring (?or for Epigonos), I*

guard the acropolis of the people of Korsiai'. In the façade of
the church, just to the right of the door, is part of an ancient dedicatory inscription 'to Hermes'. These disparate
elements are hard to link into a coherent whole.

Four hundred metres below the church of the Panaghia, a fork (4.5km) to the left leads down (1km) to the
protected and delightful **bay of Koumará** with a sandy
beach, some shade (rare on Foúrni) afforded by the trees
behind the waterfront, and the tiny **church of the Evangelistria**, set back above the shore. Beyond the Koumará
junction, the road (now considerably rougher) descends
and crosses the narrow waist of the island into its northern sector, passing the bay of **Valí** to the west. The landscape from here on is mostly barren and shadeless, coming to life only during the flowering of the spring months.

At (9.6km) the road divides: the right branch leads
down (1.2km) to the eastern shore at **Kamari**, the tiny
harbour for crossing to the island and **monastery of
Aghios Minás** opposite. The few resident inhabitants
of the scattered community are mostly employed in the
fish farm in the straits between the two islands. Set back
from the shore to the northwest above the village is the
church of Aghios Nikolaos, where, ranged in its precinct
to the east and south, are nearly a **dozen ancient columns and stones** in several materials—a lightly veined

and coloured marble, some white marble from the quarry at Petrokopió, and one column in Ikarian grey granite. These possess the shape and proportions of ancient pieces rather than of Early Christian architectural elements. They point to the existence of a settlement here, probably in Roman times, some of which is now submerged in the sea, and which must have been connected with the crossing point to the island of Aghios Minás.

From the junction above Kamari, the rough and shadeless road continues high along the ridge—offering dramatic views to Mt. Kerketéus on Samos—for a further 5.5km to **Chrysomiliá**, banked steeply in a ravine high up above the shore. The setting of the town is enviable: the mountain masses behind protect it from the north winds; there are fine views to Ikaría; there is plenty of water, and the village is unexpectedly green. The winding 1.7km road that separates the harbour of Kambi below from the main village, passes the **church of Aghia Triada**, shortly below Chrysomiliá to the south. The low church sits on a terrace constructed of finely cut isodomic blocks of local marble from the quarries at Petrokopió. These appear to have belonged to a sizeable Hellenistic tower on this site—evidence of the antiquity of this tiny and remote settlement. The waterfront of Kambi has a pebbled strand of limpid water, backed by trees. The road to Chrysomiliá can be tiring to drive or to walk (3.5–4 hours). The best means of approach is by local caïque from Foúrni (Chora): it was, until 15 years ago, the only method of reaching this isolated corner of the island.

SOUTH TO AGHIOS IOANNIS THERMASTIS

At 2.2km from Foúrni harbour, and 600m along the road to Aghios Ioannis Thermastís from the main junction above the town, an unsurfaced road leads down the mountainside to the right. The junction is at a very panoramic point, high above **Elidaki Bay**. In the hillside, not far below the main road, are the remains of a **large marble quarry**: the main cut in the hill is clearly visible. The quarry can be entered by taking the unsurfaced road which branches off to the right and doubling back down a path towards the area after a short distance. It would appear that the quarry was opened in Antiquity and has been worked sporadically until recently: there are the remains of later **quarry workers' houses** on the hillside opposite. The different areas of running striations, which in places vary slightly according to tools and methods, mark the successive campaigns of cutting down the vertical quarry face. The marble produced is of a clear white quality, and the darker surface of the quarry face is caused simply by natural patination. In some way, this site must have produced a different and preferred quality of marble to that of Petrokopió, which is a short distance beyond in the next bay: this is the only way to explain the continued use of a quarry which presented far greater logistical difficulties than Petrokopió, which was down at the shore and therefore substantially easier for transport and loading. From here, the long winding 'piste' or road which connected the quarry to the loading area and barges down at the shore—and which can still be traced on the left side of the valley between the quarry and the bay, even though it is now much overgrown—was the laborious route for transporting the cut stone.

Following the branch road south and east down the mountainside into the next bay along (1km), the ***ancient quarry of Petrokopió**, with its abandoned shipments of cut stone on the beach, soon comes into view—clear and gleaming like an image from a painting by De Chirico. This is one of the best-preserved and most instructive ancient quarries in the Aegean area—fascinating and moving even for the non-specialist, for the picture it gives of ancient industry. The quarry itself is large and divided into two principal zones by a sharp wedge-like projection of natural rock. The signs of working, and the sharply shelving ledges are visible on all sides. The latest area to be opened would appear to be just outside the main quarry to the seaward side. At the entrance on the shore below are the abandoned pieces awaiting shipment—**column drums, capitals, a large sarcophagus** (unhollowed), corner elements for an **architrave**—all stacked together to one side. They do not yet have any of the detailed carving which they would have been given at their final site: their contours have been softened by wind erosion. Some distance away, in the rocky north corner of the bay is a single column drum (visible as you descend the last few metres of the road): this may indicate that the blocks were rafted over to this point to be loaded in the greater depth of water here which better accommodated the draught of the barges. The marble of Petrokopió has a very pure and vein-less white colour, but with an icier and slightly more bluish tinge to it than Naxiot and Parian marble. It patinates naturally, however, with a warm, rosy ochre colour, which can be observed here in the quarry, as well as in the marble sarcophagus in the *plateia* of Foúrni town. This was a large and productive quarry, and much of the marble which came from it was used in buildings in Ephesus. The **beach** is composed solely of naturally smoothed and bleached pebbles of this pure and crystalline material.

After returning to the main road, it is a further kilometre around the slopes of Mt Vardia, to the church of **Aghios**

Ioannis Theologos (3.3km), situated amongst windswept tamarisks, on a narrow ridge with views out to sea both to east and west. A large sloping, stone-paved apron in front of the church collects rain-water in an underground cistern and serves also as a winnowing area, taking advantage of the ever-present cross-winds at this point.

At (6km) the road south ends at the tiny fishing village of **Aghios Ioannis Thermastís** at the head of a sheltered bay. One kilometre east of here, across the southern headland of the island, is **Vitsilia Bay** with a secluded shingle beach.

Thýmaina which faces Foúrni to the west, is sparsely inhabited and little visited. The island takes its name from the abundance of aromatic wild thyme, whose smell at times fills the atmosphere. Its harbour is particularly sheltered; the tiny settlement above the jetty is grouped around the parallel churches of Aghios Nikolaos and Aghios Ioannis Theologos: the community's tiny cemetery is at the southern end of the harbour-bay. There are no tavernas or licensed rooms for rent—only a small food store. The walk up the eastern side of Mt. Tsimbes to the hermitage of Aghios Giorgios, affords beautiful views of Foúrni and the sea beyond especially towards sunset. The F/B *Samos Spirit* runs between Foúrni and Thýmaina twice weekly on its way to and from Ikaría and Samos.

PRACTICAL INFORMATION

831 00 **Samos** & 832 00 **Karlóvasi**: area 476sq km; perimeter 159 km; resident population 41,850; max. altitude 1,434m. **Port Authority**: T. 22730 27890, 27318 (Vathý);T. 22730 61225 (Pythagóreio); T. 22730 32343, 30888 (Karlóvasi). **Travel and information**: www.samos.gr; By Ship Travel, T. 22730 25065 (Vathý), 61061 (Pythagóreio), 92341 (Kokkari), 37100 (Marathókambos) & 35252 (Karlóvasi).

83 000 **Ikaría**: area 255sq km; perimeter 107km; resident population 7,550; max. altitude 1,037m. **Port Authorities**: Aghios Kírykos 22750 22207; Evdilos 22750 31007. **Travel and information**: Municpality of Aghios Kírykos 22750 24047; Nas Travel, 22750 71396, www.island-ikaria.com

83 400 **Foúrni**: area 30sq km; perimeter 74 km; resident population 1,333; max. altitude 514m. **Port Authority**: 22750 51207. **Information**: Foúrni Municpality, T. 22750 51366.

ACCESS

By air: Domestic flights to **Samos** are frequent from Athens—4 to 5 times daily with Olympic Air and twice a day in summer with Aegean Airlines. There are also direct flights by charter from destinations outside of Greece.

 Ikaría now has a small airport at the eastern tip of the island, connected to Athens by a mid-afternoon flight every day, except on Mondays: an airport transfer bus connects flights with Ag. Kírykos 11km away.

By boat: Sea access to **Samos** is also plentiful, but a little confusing because it is split between three separate ports: **Karlóvasi** and **Vathý**, on the north coast, for the larger ferries plying the northern and western routes to Piraeus, Chios, Lesbos, Ikaría, Thessaloniki etc; and **Pythagóreio**, on the south coast, for the Dodecanese and southern routes, i.e. the F/B *Nisos Kalymnos* (4 days per week) and hydrofoils (daily) to Patmos, Lipsi, Leros, Kalymnos, Kos, and on to Rhodes, with the *Nisos Kalymnos* stopping at Agathonisi and Arki in addition, before calling at Patmos. The summer hydrofoil service to **Foúrni** and **Ikaría** (4 times weekly) also leaves from Pythagóreio. Crossings to Turkey (Kuşadası) run daily from **Vathý**, during the summer season only

(Easter–mid-October); thereafter more infrequently.

For **Ikaría**, ferries between Piraeus and Samos serve both of the island's two ports—Evdilos, on the north coast, almost daily, by either fast (5hrs, summer only, from Piraeus) or slow (8–9hrs, year-round) boats; and Aghios Kírykos, on the south coast, with 3 connections a week on the Samos–Piraeus route. The F/B *Samos Spirit* also stops at Ag. Kírykos on its way between Samos and Foúrni 3 times a week; and in the summer there are fast, *Flying Dolphin* hydrofoil connections (1hr) to and from Pythagóreio on Samos, 4 times weekly, dropping to 2 weekly for the half-season months of Apr, May, September and October. Caïques leave Ag. Kírykos most afternoons during the summer for Foúrni, and on Mon, Wed and Fri for Manganitis and Karkinágri, at the western extremity of the island.

A local caïque runs from **Foúrni** to Ikaría (Ag. Kyrikos) in the morning and returns in the afternoon fairly regularly throughout the week in summer, but less frequently in winter. *Flying Dolphin* hydrofoils also link Foúrni with Ikaría and Samos (Pythagóreio) 4 times weekly (journey time, 1hr) in high summer (July–mid Sept) and twice weekly between mid-Apr and mid-Oct only. The F/B *Samos Spirit* car ferry connects Foúrni twice weekly to Ikaría and Samos (Karlóvasi and Vathý) throughout the year: it also stops at Thýmaina 10 mins after leaving Foúrni, and represents the most regular service between the two islands. There is a twice-weekly ferry service to Piraeus.

LODGING

Samos's most civilised and unpretentious place to stay is the **Armonia Bay Hotel** (*Apr–Oct; T. 22730 92279, www.armoniabay.gr*) above Tsamadoú beach, just west of Kokkári on the north coast: it strikes a perfect balance between style, comfort and simplicity, at a contained price. In the centre of Vathý, the **Hotel Avlí**, (*also Apr–Oct; T. 22730 22939*), built around an attractive courtyard is charming and has simple rooms. Pythagóreio is problematic both because of a general erosion of quality due to the demands of mass tourism and because of nocturnal noise; it is best avoided as a place to stay. If circumstances necessitate, however, **Areli Studios** (*May–Oct; T. 22730 61245, fax 62320*) is a pleasant hotel in a garden setting, set a little way back from the harbour. At the southwestern corner of the island, in beautiful seclusion and with great style, is **Limnionas Village**, in the bay of that name (*T. 22730 37274, www.limnionas.net*);

these are self-catering cottages on weekly lets.

Ikaría's nicest hotels are not to be found in either of the ports. At Therma, the **Agriólykos Pension** (*T. 22750 22433 & 22383, www.island-ikaria.com/hotels/agriolykos.asp*), very quiet and set in a delightful garden of tamarisks with wide views, is at the top of a flight of steps above the north end of the bay. Rooms are small and simple but have air conditioning. (*Note: access is only by foot, and bags will need to be carried up to the hotel.*) In Therma town, the **Anthemis Hotel** (*T. 22750 23156 & 23377*) is simple with adequate rooms, and has helpful and friendly owners. Both hotels are inexpensive. The island's smarter hotels are mostly in the area of Armenistís: the **Hotel Erofili Beach** (*T. 22750 71058–9, www.erofili.gr*: upper price range) has large, comfortable, and well-appointed rooms overlooking the sea front and the pool: it is a good hotel, but the breakfast is somewhat disappointing and the reception decidedly cool. Just outside Armenistís, on the way to Nas is the charming **Hotel Daidalos** (*T 22750 71390–2*), looking west out to sea: next door to it, and of equivalent standard but more old-fashioned, is the **Cavos Bay Hotel** (*T. 22750 71381-3, www.cavosbay.com.gr*). Both of the above are in the medium price range. Those seeking real peace and quiet might explore **Tzamoudakis Rooms** in remote Karkinágri (*T. 22750 91217 & 91327*).

Lodging on **Foúrni** is plentiful but basic. The nearest thing to an hotel is **Toula's** (*T. 22750 51332*) on the waterfront just south of the ferry jetty: but a number of the houses with rooms to let in the town have greater character. **Maria's Rooms** (*T. 22750 51204*) in one of the houses on the south side of the main street with an older style façade, are pleasantly appointed and offer a balcony for watching the evening *volta*.

EATING

On **Samos**, at Vathý, **Christos** (two blocks in from the water-front, and north of the main square) serves Asia Minor specialties, interesting salads, and good fragrant wine. The village of Vourliotes has several tavernas offering good, mountain food in its picturesque *plateia*: less contrived, and more popular with islanders, is **Pera Vrysi**, at the entrance to the village. On the shore below, at Avlákia, the **Mezedopoleío 'Doña Rosa'** has a pleasing touch of eccentricity, but nonetheless prepares excellent Greek dishes with local ingredients and good presentation. Further west at Palaio

Karlóvasi, the **Oinomageir-eío 'Dryousa'**, in the *plateia* where the paved road ends, is family-run, providing fresh, home cooking. The last true tavernas in Pythagóreio closed some time ago; the best remaining eatery there, with a pleasant view from its position at the beginning of the harbour mole, is **Varka**. For sunset views, however, few can match **Balkoni tou Aigeiou** at the south end of Spatherei; while the taverna at Koutsi, up and west from Pyrgos, though not remarkable for food, is an unforgettable and cool refuge on a hot day, beside a spring below plane trees in the hills of central Samos. Pure comb honey of high quality can be found at *Melissa*—a small supply-shop, a few metres up the main street of Pythagóreio, from the harbour.

On **Ikaría**, for a variety of local and traditional dishes always freshly prepared, Christos Chazálas's **Taverna 'To tzaki'**, in Glaredo (2km west of Ag. Kírykos) is much to be recommended; in Ag. Kírykos itself, the tiny **Taverna Klimataria**, under a vine pergola, a couple of blocks in from the harbour, serves good soups and oven dishes, and is justly favoured by locals for its good value. There are several good tavernas at Kato Ráches overlooking the site at Nas: **Taverna 'O Nas'** has the best view, but the food is more imaginative and homemade in character at **Anna's Taverna**. In Karkinágri, the fresh fish is generally excellent at **Perkas Restaurant**.

Building on the fame of **Foúrni's** lobster-fishing fleet, the two main restaurants on the waterfront, **Nikos** (or more properly 'Taverna Remezzo') and **Miltos** are popular and full with locals and visitors alike; both have undoubtedly good fish-dishes and are comparable in price and quality. What they may lack in the homely touch can be found, however, inland along the main street under the mulberries, where **To koutouki tou Psaradikou** specializes in traditional, homemade oven dishes, such as *papoutsaki* (stuffed aubergine) and *briam* (a kind of Greek ratatouille). **O Kalokardos**, beside the town's main church of Ag. Nikolaos, is good for local wine and specialises in meat dishes. The fish taverna at Kamari is popular with islanders in the summer; likewise the little taverna **Pilavaki** in Chrysomilia.

WINE

Of the variety of Samian wines produced by the island's Wine-making Co-operative, the dry *Arousa* (12%) and the sweet *Phyllás* (15%)—coincidentally by the same producer—are to be recommended for consistency, quality and purity, as well as for their

interest to the nose and
palate.

FURTHER READING

Samos
Graham Shipley, *A History of Samos 800–188 BC* (Oxford University Press, 1987); Hermann Kienast, *The Aqueduct of Eupalinos* (*Greek Ministry of Culture, Athens, 2005*).

INDEX

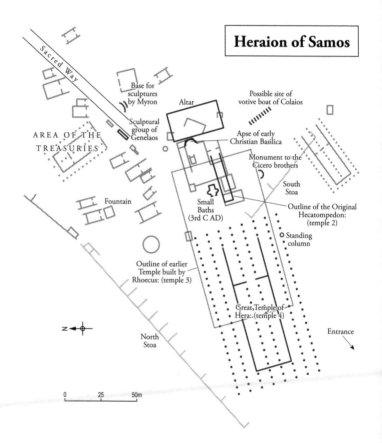

Heraion of Samos

Sacred Way

Base for sculptures by Myron

Sculptural group of Genelaos

AREA OF THE TREASURIES

Altar

Possible site of votive boat of Colaios

Apse of early Christian Basilica

Monument to the Cicero brothers

South Stoa

Outline of the Original Hecatompedon: (temple 2)

Fountain

Small Baths (3rd C AD)

Standing column

Outline of earlier Temple built by Rhoecus: (temple 3)

Great Temple of Hera: (temple 4)

Entrance

N

North Stoa

0   25   50m

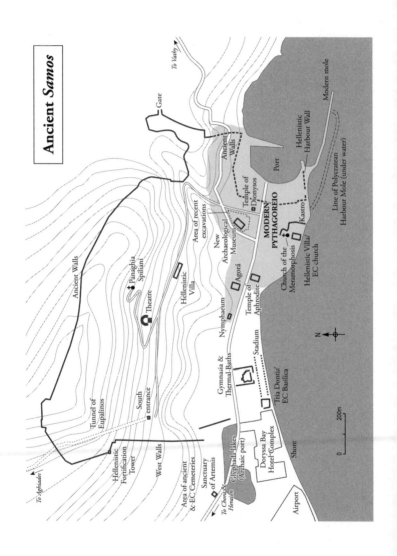

Ancient *Samos*

To Vathy

Gate

Modern mole

Ancient Walls

Hellenistic Harbour Wall

Port

Temple of Dionysos

Area of recent excavations

Line of Polycratean Harbour Mole (under water)

New Archaeological Museum

MODERN PYTHAGOREIO

Kastro

Ancient Walls

Panaghia Spiliani

Theatre

Hellenistic Villa

Agorá

Church of the Metamorphosis

Hellenistic Villa/ EC church

Nymphaeum

Temple of Aphrodite

Tunnel of Eupalinos

South entrance

Stadium

N

Gymnasia & Thermal-Baths

'Tria Dontia' EC Basilica

Hellenistic Fortification Tower

West Walls

Shore

200m

0

To Aghiades

Area of ancient & EC Cemeteries

Doryssa Bay Hotel 'Complex'

Glyphadi-lakes (Archaic port)

Sanctuary of Artemis

Airport

To Chora & Heraion